T0082433

REEDS
SKIPPER'S
HANDBOOK

REEDS SKIPPER'S HANDBOOK

FOR SAIL AND POWER

8th edition

ANDY DU PORT
and MALCOLM PEARSON

REEDS

LONDON • OXFORD • NEW YORK • NEW DELHI • SYDNEY

REEDS
Bloomsbury Publishing Plc
50 Bedford Square, London, WC1B 3DP, UK
29 Earlsfort Terrace, Dublin 2, Ireland

BLOOMSBURY, REEDS and the Reeds logo are trademarks of Bloomsbury Publishing Plc
First published in 1993 by Thomas Reed Publications
Second edition 1995
Revised 1998
Third edition 2000
Reprinted 2002
Fourth edition published by Adlard Coles Nautical 2004
Fifth edition 2007
Sixth edition 2010
Seventh edition 2020
This edition 2024

A catalogue record for this book is available from the British Library.
ISBN: 978-1-3994-1429-6; ePub: 978-1-3994-1427-2; ePDF: 978-1-3994-1428-9

2 4 6 8 10 9 7 5 3 1

Typeset in Myriad Pro Light 9/11pt by Carrdesignstudio.com

MIX
Paper | Supporting
responsible forestry
FSC® C004800
www.fsc.org

Printed in UAE by Oriental Press

To find out more about our authors and books visit www.bloomsbury.com
and sign up for our newsletters.

CONTENTS

Introduction

This 8th edition of the *Reeds Skipper's Handbook* has been largely rewritten, but it is based on the original work by Malcolm Pearson in 1993.

Much has changed in the last 30 years, most significantly the introduction of GPS and electronic charting systems which have revolutionised navigation in small craft and, indeed, in all seagoing vessels. Many large ships, with their multiple back-up systems, no longer carry paper charts at all. It is tempting to do the same in our yachts but lack of space and the vulnerability of electronic devices to damp and accidental damage mean that paper charts will earn their place on board for many years to come.

To use paper charts effectively, basic navigational skills need to be preserved: taking and plotting visual fixes, working up an estimated position (EP) and making decisions based on the results. *Reeds Skipper's Handbook* therefore focuses on this while acknowledging that electronic systems can make life simpler, less stressful and often navigationally more precise.

However, nothing can replace good seamanship displayed by a knowledgeable and experienced skipper, but we all have moments when our memory fails and we need a ready reference to check up on a simple fact or figure. This book fulfils that need. Collision avoidance, rules of the road, weather forecasting, tides, boat handling and much more are all covered.

One major reduction in this edition is the section on UK inland waterways. Most seagoing yachts don't venture far up rivers or into our canal system. For those who do, far more detailed and authoritative guidance can be obtained from the Canal & River Trust and the Environment Agency.

The section on European waterways and CEVNI is largely unchanged.

Finally, remember: *'A bad day sailing is 100 times better than a good day at work.'*

Andy Du Port

Acknowledgements

In recognition of the leading part played by the RYA in the promotion of safe practice for recreational boaters, it should be noted that many of the techniques explained in this book emanate from the RYA and are those routinely taught by RYA trained instructors to students enrolled on their navigation and seamanship courses.

This product has been derived in part from material obtained from the UK Hydrographic Office, His Majesty's Stationery Office.

Figures on pages 12, 41, 42, 43, 54, 58, 59, 64 and 68 © British Crown Copyright, 2024. All rights reserved.

The life-saving signals on pages 135–6 are based on material issued by the MCA and are reproduced with their kind permission.

Thanks to *Practical Boat Owner* for permission to reproduce material previously published in that magazine.

NOTE: Every effort has been made to find the copyright holders of any material used in this book that is not the author's own.

Latitude and longitude

In the absence of visible points of reference when out of sight of land, positions at sea are expressed in terms of *latitude* (your distance north or south of the equator) and *longitude* (your distance east or west of the Greenwich meridian) (*Fig 1*).

Latitude is 0° at the equator and 90° at the poles. For all practical purposes 1° of latitude equals 60 nautical miles (NM), so one sixtieth of a degree – one minute – is 1NM (*Fig 2*).

Longitude is 0° at the Greenwich meridian to 180° east or west. Thus a longitude of 180° (W or E) on the equator is in the middle of the Pacific Ocean. As the meridians, also known as *lines of longitude*, converge at the poles, 1° of longitude at the equator represents 60NM but reduces to zero at the poles (*Fig 3*).

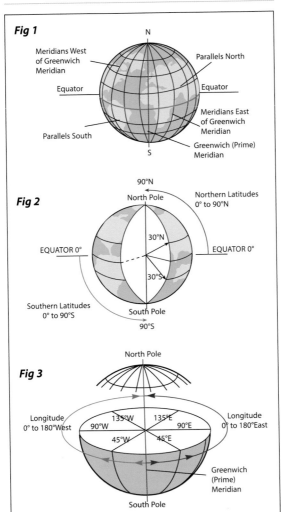

Fig 1

Meridians West
of Greenwich
Meridian

Parallels North

Equator

Equator

Meridians East
of Greenwich
Meridian

Parallels South

Greenwich (Prime)
Meridian

N

S

Fig 2

90°N
North Pole

Northern Latitudes
0° to 90°N

30°N

EQUATOR 0°

EQUATOR 0°

30°S

Southern Latitudes
0° to 90°S

South Pole

90°S

Fig 3

North Pole

Longitude
0° to 180°West

135°W   135°E

90°W   90°E

45°W   45°E

Longitude
0° to 180°East

Greenwich
(Prime)
Meridian

South Pole

Positions

Positions are given in degrees and minutes of latitude followed by degrees and minutes of longitude. If greater accuracy is required, tenths (or even hundredths) of a minute may be shown.

For instance, Nelson's Column in London is in position 51° 30'·47N, 000° 07'·68W. Note that degrees of latitude are shown as two figures (4°N would be shown as 04°N) and degrees of longitude as three figures, as in the example above. Similarly, minutes are shown as two figures with the minutes symbol (') before the decimal point.

As one minute of latitude represents 1NM, 0.1 minutes is roughly 185 metres and 0.01 minutes about 18 metres – a measure of accuracy not often required at sea.

Because the Earth is not a perfect sphere, one minute of latitude is 1843 metres at the equator and 1862 metres at the poles, a difference of just 19 metres. By international agreement, the *nautical mile* (NM) is defined as the average of the two: 1852 metres (6076 feet).

The latitude scales on nautical charts are shown in *sea miles* (which take into account the shape of the Earth) but for navigational purposes they are the same as nautical miles.

A tenth of a nautical mile is a *cable*, so 0.6NM could also be expressed as 6 cables.

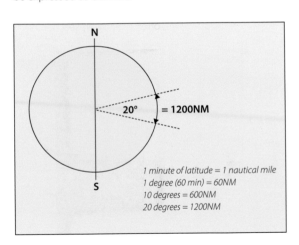

1 minute of latitude = 1 nautical mile
1 degree (60 min) = 60NM
10 degrees = 600NM
20 degrees = 1200NM

Chart projections

To show the spherical Earth on a flat chart requires it to be 'projected'. A light inside a transparent globe would cause shadows to be projected on a nearby wall, but the shapes of landmasses would be significantly distorted.

Most charts are produced using *Mercator projection*. This allows the meridians to be parallel, and any track drawn on the chart will be a straight line, crossing all meridians at the same angle – and thus the same course. This is fine for relatively short distances, but for ocean passages of more than a few hundred miles it would not be the shortest route.

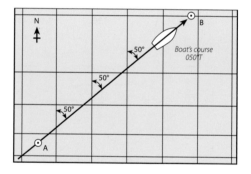

Gnomonic charts are used for planning long passages when a *great circle* track is required (see below). On a *Gnomonic chart* the track is shown as a straight line but cuts the meridians at different angles.

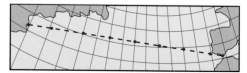

Great circles and rhumb lines

A *great circle* is the largest circle which can be drawn on the surface of a sphere. The equator is a great circle, as are all meridians of longitude. The shortest distance between any two points is the great circle which joins them.

For example, although Norfolk, USA, is almost exactly due west of Gibraltar, an aeroplane flying between the two will leave Gibraltar on a north-westerly course and approach Norfolk from the northeast. It will be flying a *great circle route* to save distance (and fuel). To achieve this the aeroplane would ideally fly a constantly changing course to maintain its track. In practice, and certainly at sea, the navigator picks off a series of coordinates from the great circle track and steers a *rhumb line* between them.

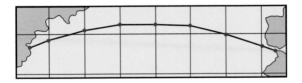

A *rhumb line* crosses all meridians at the same angle and is shown as a straight line on a Mercator chart. Although not the shortest distance between two points, it is perfectly adequate for coastal and short offshore passages, except in the high latitudes.

Measuring distance

To measure distance on a Mercator chart, the latitude scale on the sides of the chart must be used, not the longitude scales at top and bottom. One minute of latitude equates to 1NM in any direction. Because the scale changes with latitude, the most accurate measurements will be made by using the scale adjacent to your area of interest.

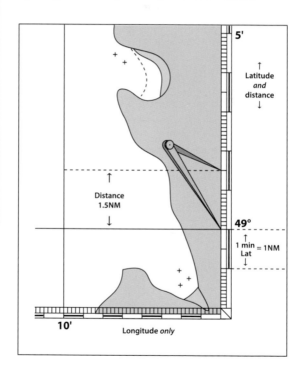

5'

↑
Latitude
and
distance
↓

↑
Distance
1.5NM
↓

49°

↑
1 min = 1NM
Lat
↓

10'   Longitude *only*

Plotting tracks and positions

To plot a position on a chart, or to find the latitude and longitude of a charted object, use a pair of dividers to measure the latitude on the side of the chart, and longitude on the top or bottom.

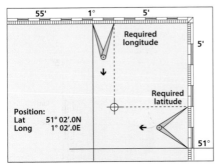

Position on the Earth's surface is expressed in terms of latitude and longitude.

To draw a track or to find the bearing of one point from another, use a straight edge and slide it across to the nearest compass rose. For greater accuracy, use a parallel ruler with hinges or rollers. Even easier to use is a Portland Course Plotter, often called a Breton Plotter. Place an edge of the plotter along the track, or between the two points, rotate the graticule north-south, and read of the bearing (or course).

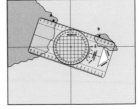

Portland Plotters also have a scale which enables variation (see pages 23–4) to be taken into account.

Chart symbols

Most producers of nautical charts use the same symbology as the UKHO. Where there are differences, they are invariably explained on the chart or on a separate sheet.

Some of the commonly used symbols are shown below. A complete list is available from the UKHO (Chart 5011).

	Overfalls, tide rips, races
	Eddies
Obstn Obstn	Obstruction or danger, exact nature not specified or determined, depth unknown
4_6 Obstn	Obstruction, depth known
4_6 Obstn	Obstruction which has been swept by wire to the depth shown
5_8 19 18 Br	Breakers
(3·1) (1·7) (·41)	Rock which does not cover, height above high water
(1_6) (1_6) (5_8)	Rock which covers and uncovers, height above chart datum
	Rock awash at the level of chart datum
	Underwater rock, depth unknown, considered dangerous to surface navigation
Wk	Wreck showing any part of hull or superstructure at the level of chart datum
	Wreck, depth unknown which is considered dangerous to surface navigation
Mast (1·2) Masts Funnel Mast (1_2)	Wreck of which the mast(s) only are visible at chart datum

A complete list of symbols and abbreviations is provided in the Admiralty publication Chart 5011.

Buoys and marks

The **IALA Region A** system of buoyage is used around the coasts of UK and Europe. The **IALA Region B** system is used in other parts of the world, notably North and South America. The only difference concerns lateral marks: IALA A has red marks to port when entering harbour, IALA B has green marks to port.

IALA used to stand for the **I**nternational **A**ssociation of **L**ighthouse **A**uthorities. It now stands for the rather less catchy International Association of Marine Aids to Navigation and Lighthouse Authorities.

The following pages show the various buoys and other marks associated with IALA A. They fall into seven categories:

Lateral marks These define the limits of navigable channels when approaching from seaward (generally in the direction of the flood tidal stream), red to port, green to starboard. Where this is not obvious, or where the direction changes, a *direction of buoyage* symbol is used:

Cardinal marks The colours and topmarks indicate the 4 quadrants: north, south, east and west. They are placed according to the danger they are marking. Thus a north cardinal mark should be passed to the north, a west mark passed to the west etc. The logic of these marks is:

♦ Topmarks point to the relevant direction: both cones up for north, down for south, towards each other for west ('wine glass' shape) and away from each other for east.

Buoys and marks

* *Black section(s)* of the mark itself corresponds to the topmarks (top for north etc).
* *Light characteristics* conform with a clock face: 3 flashes for east, 6 + 1 long flash for south, 9 for west and continuous flashing for north. The reason for the long flash on a south mark and the continuous flashing on a north mark is to avoid any ambiguity with the other lights.

Preferred channel marks Used to mark the preferred or main channel where a channel divides.

Isolated danger marks Mark an isolated danger which has safe water all round it.

Safe water marks Used in open water to indicate, for example, the start of a fairway.

Special marks Of no navigational significance, they mark areas of interest such as spoil grounds and watersports areas. They are often used as yacht racing marks.

Wreck marks Deployed to mark a new wreck until it can be permanently marked (usually with cardinal marks).

Cardinal marks

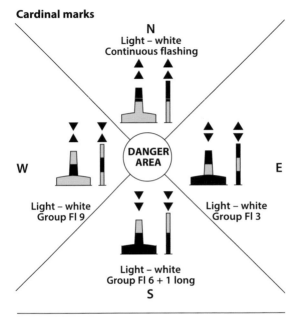

N
Light – white
Continuous flashing

W

DANGER AREA

E

Light – white
Group Fl 9

Light – white
Group Fl 3

Light – white
Group Fl 6 + 1 long

S

Isolated danger mark

Danger with safe water all round
Light – white Group Fl 2

Safe water mark

Safe deepwater all round
Light – white. Occulting, isophase,
or 1 long flash or Morse 'A'
Pass either side, but leave to
port when entering or leaving
a channel entrance

Lateral marks – region 'A'

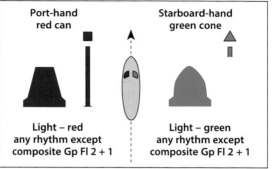

Port-hand
red can

Starboard-hand
green cone

Light – red
any rhythm except
composite Gp Fl 2 + 1

Light – green
any rhythm except
composite Gp Fl 2 + 1

Preferred channel marks (modified lateral marks)

Main channel
to starboard

Main channel
to Port

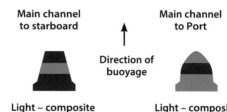

Direction of
buoyage

Light – composite
Gp Fl 2 + 1 red

Light – composite
Gp Fl 2 +1 green

Special marks

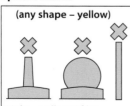

(any shape – yellow)

Light – yellow (if lit)

Any rhythm other than those
prescribed for cardinal, isolated
danger or safe water marks

'New hazard' mark

Light – alt. blue/yellow

Emergency wreck marking
buoy – deployed in the
initial period following a
wreckage

Light characteristics

The flashing sequence of lights fall into six main categories:

Fixed – F – Continuous, steady light

Flashing – Fl – May be single flashes or multiple flashes separated by a period of darkness

Morse – Mo (U) – Morse code sequence (Uniform in this example)

Occulting – Oc – A steady light which is off (dark) for brief periods, single or multiple

Isophase – Equal periods of light and dark

Alternating – Al (WR) – Shows a different colour in successive flashes (white and red in this example)

Lights may also be **sectored**, showing different colours when viewed from different directions.

Light characteristics	Int abbr	Period shown

Fixed *A continuous steady light*

F

Occulting *Steady light – eclipsed at regular and repeated intervals*

Single

Oc

Group

Oc (2)

Isophase *Duration – light and dark equal*

Iso

Flashing *Single flashes at regular intervals. Duration of light less than dark*

Single

Fl

Long

L Fl

Group

Fl (3)

Composite group

Fl (2 + 1)

Morse code

Mo (K)

Alternating *Light which alters colour*

Al WR

in successive flashes

W   R   W   R   W

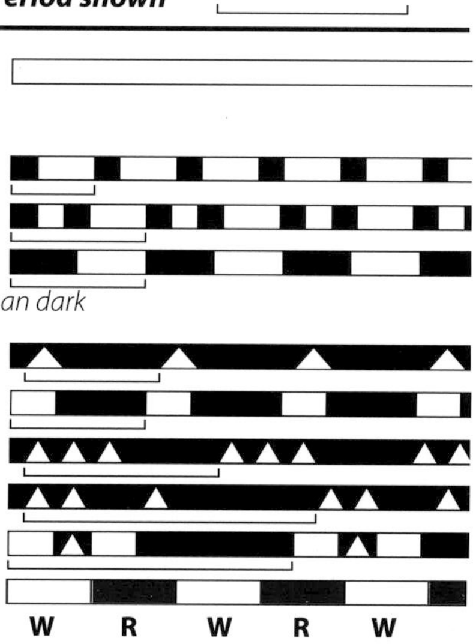

Sectored light *Shows different colour light when viewed from*

Electronic navigational charts

Nautical charts loaded into a chart plotter, or downloaded onto a laptop, tablet or phone will be in one of two formats:

Raster Electronic copies of paper charts. They may be magnified or reduced in size (zoom in/out), but the detail remains exactly the same.

Vector Digitised versions of the original charts which are built up in layers: sea bed, depth contours, buoyage etc. What you see depends on the scale in use. When zoomed out (small scale) only basic data will be available; when zoomed in (large scale) all details will be seen.

It is important when passage planning or navigating in restricted waters, therefore, to zoom in along your intended track or area of interest to be sure of spotting potential hazards which may not show at smaller scales.

Chart corrections

Rocks may not move, but other details shown on charts certainly do. Sandbanks shift, light characteristics change, buoys are repositioned and new infrastructure is built. It is essential, therefore, that charts are kept up to date. This is not difficult to do yourself, and there are several sources of information:

- The UKHO produces Notices to Mariners (NtMs) which may be viewed online or downloaded at no cost.
- Imray (and others) issue corrections to their own charts.
- Harbour authorities issue Local Notices to Mariners (LNtM).
- *Reeds Nautical Almanac* and *The Cruising Almanac* publish amendments which can be related to the relevant charts.

Many corrections can be safely ignored by small craft navigators. Changes of depths over about 10 metres, for instance, are of little interest to yachts, and it is entirely up to you which corrections you deem to be relevant. That said, it is wise to trawl through all corrections to make sure nothing of importance is missed.

There are no hard and fast rules about plotting chart corrections, but they do need to be clear and unambiguous. Some examples are shown below.

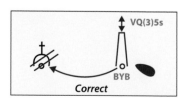

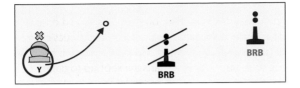

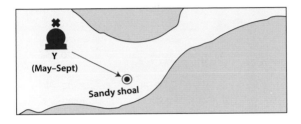

Electronic charts cannot be corrected directly by the user, but the supplier may either reprogram a removable cartridge (for chart plotters) or issue downloadable updates (for laptops and tablets). It is advisable to check that corrections shown in NtMs are fully and accurately reflected in your electronic system or app.

Introduction

A magnetic compass does not rely on any power supply or external electronic signals. It is a truly independent means of determining direction and heading. When all else fails, you may need to rely on it to keep safe and find your way back to harbour. Its accuracy, however, is influenced in two significant ways: *variation* and *deviation*.

A magnetic compass points to magnetic north, but the magnetic north pole is constantly moving and can be several thousand miles from the geographic North Pole. Variation is the angular difference between magnetic north and true north, and varies according to your location. It is expressed in degrees east or west of true north. Around the UK it is currently (2023) between 0° and 4°. In some parts of the world variation can be 40° or even more.

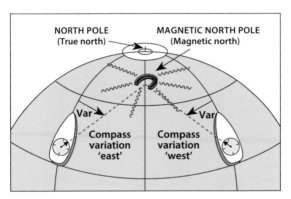

A magnetic compass points towards magnetic north, not true north. Variation is the angular difference between them.

Variation is shown on the compass roses on paper charts, along with its annual rate of change. It can also be found, for instance, on the area maps in *Reeds Nautical Almanac*.

THE MAGNETIC COMPASS

Applying variation

Having found the variation in your location, you need to apply an appropriate correction to your compass to find true north. If the variation is **west** (of true north), you must **subtract** it from the compass bearing. Conversely, if the variation is **east**, it must be **added** to the compass bearing. This can be remembered by the mnemonic **CADET**:

Compass **AD**d **E**ast to get **T**rue

So, if the variation is 3°W, a *compass* bearing of 135° would be a *true* bearing of 132° (135° **minus** 3°).

To allow for variation when determining a course to steer by compass, the reverse holds true. For the same variation of 3°W, to steer a *true* course of 240° you need to steer a *compass* course of 243° (135° **plus** 3°).

A magnetic compass is also, not surprisingly, affected by ferrous materials close to it. In a yacht it should be sited where it can best be seen from the helm, and a thorough audit made of ferrous and electrical equipment in the immediate vicinity. Electrical equipment which might affect the compass will have a 'compass safe distance' – usually about a metre – which should be carefully observed when it is installed.

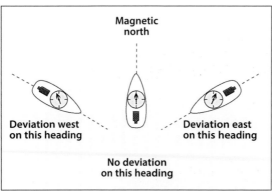

Magnetic
north

**Deviation west
on this heading**

**Deviation east
on this heading**

No deviation
on this heading

The mass of this boat's engine is influencing the compass card. Each time the course is altered, the relative positions of the engine and the compass change and so does the value of deviation on that heading.

Be aware of any loose gear which might be left near the compass. Phones, tablets and portable radios are common culprits.

Deviation will vary according to the compass heading of the vessel. You can check for deviation on the steering compass in several ways:

Deviation

- ◆ If you have a hand-bearing compass on board which can be moved where it is not affected by magnetic influences, direct comparisons can be made between it and the steering compass on various headings.
- ◆ In still water (no current or tidal stream), compare the compass headings with the course over the ground (COG) from your GPS.
- ◆ Steer accurately towards two charted objects in transit, then compare the compass heading with the **magnetic** bearing of the transit. Repeat this on other transit to build up a pattern of deviation.

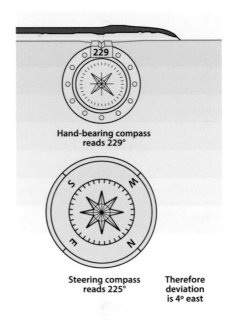

Hand-bearing compass reads 229°

Steering compass reads 225°

Therefore deviation is 4° east

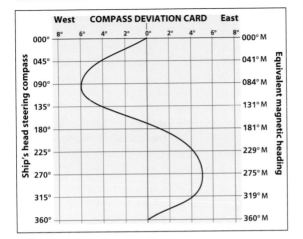

If you are concerned that your compass suffers from significant deviation – more than a few degrees – you may need to employ a qualified compass adjuster to 'swing the compass' and draw up a graph of deviation (a Compass Deviation Card) on various headings. Some yacht compasses can be adjusted to minimise deviation. If not, you will need to apply deviation in exactly the same way as for variation.

▶▶ **Note**

Deviation values are for specific compass, not true, headings.

If the combined effect of variation and deviation – the total compass error – is less than two or three degrees, it can probably be safely disregarded.

Introduction

Although you don't need to know your exact position at all times, you do need to be sure that the boat is in safe water and not heading into danger. The proximity of any hazards will dictate the degree of accuracy required and the frequency of *fixing*. However, a conscientious navigator will always endeavour to confirm the vessel's position as precisely as possible, using all means available.

It is tempting to rely entirely on GPS. It is reliable, accurate and simple to use. Your position may be displayed as a latitude and longitude or as a marker on a screen. It is essential, though, to be able to fix your position if GPS should fail, perhaps because of a malfunction of the satellite system, a fault in your receiving equipment, damage to the aerial or a power failure on board. Although the likelihood of any of these are small, you may have no option other than reverting to basic fixing and plotting techniques to keep the boat and her crew safe, and to reach a safe destination.

There are many ways of establishing your position. The fundamental input is a *position line*. This may be a visual or radar bearing of a charted object, a radar range, a range using a sextant (see page 104), a transit or a depth contour. Any of these is a line (or arc) on which you must lie. To *fix* your position, you need at least two position lines to intersect. These may be two visual bearings of different objects, a radar range and a depth contour, or any other combination.

How accurately you can take visual bearings or determine the depth of water, for example, will affect the accuracy of the resultant fix. You should therefore aim to use as many position lines as possible. Inevitably, they will not all cross at exactly the same point, so you will have to use your judgement to determine your actual position.

Compass bearings

Before you use a compass to take bearings or plot a course, you must decide if you are working with true, magnetic or compass bearings. Don't mix them or you will build in unnecessary errors. Any conversions (from magnetic to true, for example) must be done before drawing lines on the chart.

Note

True to Compass
1. True bearing ±Variation = Magnetic bearing
2. Magnetic bearing ± Deviation = Compass bearing

Add if variation or deviation is **west**
Subtract if variation or deviation is **east**

Compass to True
1. Compass bearing ± Deviation = Magnetic bearing
2. Magnetic bearing ± Variation = True bearing

Add if variation or deviation is **east**
Subtract if variation or deviation is **west**

As stated above, two bearings which intersect will theoretically give your position, but three or more will help to refine this. Follow these steps:

1. Study the chart to identify at least three objects which you can also see. They should be well spaced in order to give a good 'cut'.

The three-point fix

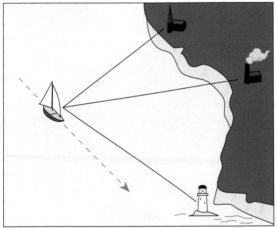

What you see.

2. Take the bearings as quickly as possible to minimise errors caused by the boat's speed over the ground. The bearing of an object on the beam will be altering the most quickly, so take it at the planned time of the fix, followed by the objects further ahead or astern. This is particularly relevant if taking bearings from a high-speed craft.

3. The resultant fix, unless you are very lucky, will be a triangle (or 'cocked hat') formed by all the position lines. The size of the cocked hat is an indication of the accuracy of the fix. It is prudent to assume the worst case, and plot your position within the cocked hat at the point closest to the nearest danger.

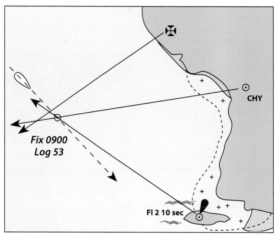

How it looks on the chart.

4. Work up an estimated position (EP) (see page 37) at least as far ahead as the time of the next planned fix. Remember that a fix is history; your actual position is somewhere further down the track.

A variation on a visual three-point visual fix is to use a *transit*. Any two objects in line are said to be in transit, and the exact bearing of one from the other can be measured on the chart. If you see two objects in line, you *must* be on a line extending from them to you. One other position line (a bearing, range or depth contour) will fix you position along that transit.

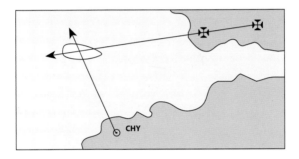

Transits

Transits are commonly used to follow an exact track, into a harbour. Special marks are often established to form a *leading line* through hazardous waters. These are very accurate, but beware of other vessels coming towards you using the same transit. One or both of you will need to move off the transit to avoid a collision, so you need to know how far you can safely go. See **clearing bearings** opposite.

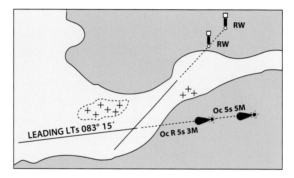

It is often possible to find a *natural transit* when there are no suitable charted objects. First, navigate your way to a point on the desired track, then look to see what objects are in transit on the bearing of the track. They can be anything: a tree in line with a telegraph pole, a house in line with a rock. The list is endless.

If no obvious transits are available when you are navigating through restricted waters you can keep safe by using *clearing bearings*. These are simply lines drawn from a prominent object (or a waypoint) which mark the boundaries of safe water. In the figure below if you keep the bearing of the chosen object less than 025° but more than 350°, you will be clear of the dangers either side. It is a matter of not knowing exactly where you are, but knowing where you are *not*!

If the bearing is *more* than planned, you must turn to *starboard*; if *less*, turn to *port*.

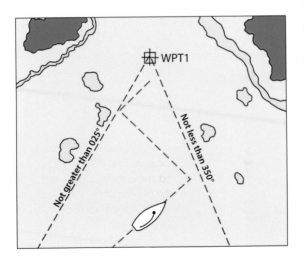

Running fix

Another variation on a visual three-point fix is a *running fix*, which uses just one charted object.

1. Take a bearing of the object **A**, noting the time and the log reading.
2. Steer a steady course.
3. Some time later, take another bearing **B**, again noting the time and log reading.
4. Plot both bearings on the chart.
5. Chose a point along bearing **A** which is close to your estimated position, then plot your track over the ground (ie your course, distance run by the log, and any tidal stream and leeway) to establish another estimated position.
6. Draw a line parallel to bearing **A** so that it passes through the new EP. Where that line intersects bearing **B** is your position at the time you took bearing **B**.

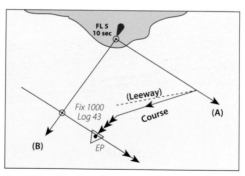

How it looks on the chart.

The accuracy of a running fix depends on how steady a course is steered between the bearings, and the actual effect of tidal stream, leeway etc.

Dead reckoning and estimated position

From the last known position, it is possible to estimate the boat's future position using just the compass for the course steered, and the log for the distance travelled through the water. This is called *dead reckoning* (DR) and is unlikely to be very accurate. It may be useful in open water when, for instance, you want a rough and ready assessment of when you will be entering a busy shipping lane.

A more accurate calculation of your position takes into account additional factors such as tidal stream, leeway, currents and anything else which may influence your course and speed over the ground. This is called an *estimated position* (EP), and is your very best guess.

Plotting the estimated position (EP)

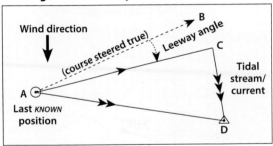

1. Decide on the starting point (**A**). Ideally, this will be your last *known* position, obtained by GPS or a visual fix. Alternatively, it will be the previously estimated position.
2. From **A** draw your course steered and distance run to **B**.
3. Refine this by adjusting for any leeway (**AC**).
4. From **C** plot the tidal stream (and current if relevant) to **D**.

Dead reckoning and estimated position

5. **D** is your estimated position, and **AD** is the course made good (CMG) and the distance travelled over the ground. From this, you can calculate speed over the ground (SOG) (distance ÷ time).

To keep things simple work up your EP at set intervals. In open waters, every hour should be fine; more frequently in restricted areas. For consistency, it is a good idea to use the standard symbology (see below).

Each EP will inevitably include some errors. If you need to estimate your position over a long period, the effect of these errors will steadily increase, and you must judge how precisely the course is steered (perhaps ± 5°), the distance logged, and the actual tidal stream/leeway. When these 'plus and minus' variations are plotted, a 'pool of errors' is formed. You should be within this area and, as with a visual fix, you should choose the point closest to danger.

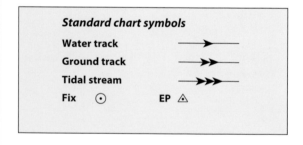

Navigational wrinkles

To end this section on position, here are a few navigational 'wrinkles':

1. **Tidal streams**. Look at the flow of water past fishing floats, buoys and other fixed objects to estimate the *actual* rate and direction. It may vary significantly from predictions.

2. **Pilotage**. A detailed sketch of the pilotage plan in a notebook saves constant trips to the chart table. Be very wary of having charts in the cockpit where they can get wet or blow away.

3. **Time and distance**. In 6 minutes (one tenth of an hour) you will cover one tenth of your speed in miles. At 6 knots you will cover 0.6NM; at 12 knots you will cover 1.2NM. In 3 minutes you will cover half the distance. This is useful when 'buoy hopping' in poor visibility.

4. **Distance off track**. 1° at 6NM subtends an arc of 1 cable (tenth of a mile). On a 60NM passage, a helming or compass error of 5° will put you 5NM from your destination.

5. **Dutchman's log**. You can measure your speed through the water by the time it takes to pass an object. Speed = $(0.592 \times \text{LOA (in feet)}) \div$ time in seconds. For a 34ft boat and a time of 5 seconds, the speed is $34 \times 0.592 \div 5 = 4$ knots. A table can be drawn up for your boat at various speeds.

Flood and ebb

Tidal streams are the horizontal movement of the water caused by the tides. Streams will therefore be greatest at springs and least at neaps.

The tidal stream *floods* as the tide rises and *ebbs* as the tide goes out. The ebb stream is almost invariably stronger than the flood and is proportional to the range of the tide. Around the time of HW and LW the stream will be *slack*, while the tide is at a *stand*.

Tidal diamonds

Where the tidal streams have been measured at a particular position over a period of time, a letter in a small diamond (◊) refers to the associated table on the chart. Here you can read off the direction and rate of the tidal stream for each hour before and after HW at the relevant standard port.

Tidal Streams referred to HW Dover

	◊A 50 42'3N 0 26'5E			◊B 50 53'0N 1 00'6E			◊C 51 01'0N 1 10'0E			◊D 51 09'7N 1 27'8E			◊D 51 03'0N 1 40'0E		
		Rate (kn)			Rate (kn)			Rate (kn)			Rate (kn)			Rate (kn)	
Hours	Dir	Sp	Np	Dir	Sp	Np	Dir	Sp	Np	Dir	Sp	Np	Dir	Sp	Np
Before HW 6	248	0.8	0.4	211	1.6	0.9	224	0.9	0.5	212	2.2	1.2	220	1.7	0.9
5	067	0.5	0.3	211	2.1	1.2	239	1.0	0.6	213	2.2	1.2	220	2.8	1.6
4	068	1.9	1.0	211	1.8	1.1	235	1.1	0.6	216	1.9	1.1	220	3.5	2.0
3	068	2.6	1.5	211	0.9	0.5	242	0.6	0.4	228	1.3	0.8	220	2.8	1.6
2	068	2.3	1.3	Slack			Slack			Slack			220	1.2	0.7
1	068	1.2	0.6	031	0.8	0.5	052	0.6	0.3	032	1.2	1.7	040	0.8	0.4
HW	067	0.1	0.1	031	1.5	0.8	049	1.2	0.7	038	2.0	1.2	040	2.5	0.1
1	248	0.9	0.5	031	1.9	1.1	049	1.3	0.7	039	2.3	1.3	040	3.4	1.9
2	247	1.4	0.8	031	1.7	1.0	156	1.0	0.5	034	2.2	1.2	040	2.9	1.6
3	247	1.4	1.0	031	1.6	1.0	159	2.3	0.4	034	1.8	1.2	040	2.5	1.4

Tidal stream tables (top) and a chart extract (below) showing tidal diamond B.

Some electronic charts show tidal arrows for the whole area on the screen. You may have to zoom in for the arrows to appear.

Tidal stream atlases

Tidal atlases show tidal streams on separate pages for each hour before and after HW. Similar chartlets can be found in almanacs, pilots and cruising companions, but these tend to be at a much smaller scale.

The arrows indicate the direction of the stream. The associated numbers show the rate of the stream in tenths of a knot at neaps and springs, while the comma between them is the actual position of the observations. Thus, → **12,45** indicates an east-going stream with a neap rate of 1.2 knots and a spring rate of 4.5 knots.

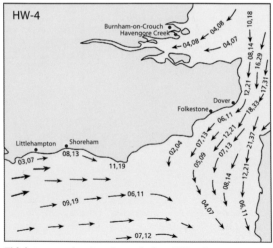

Tidal stream atlas. Four hours before HW at Dover: south-going stream in the Dover Strait meeting the flood stream in the eastern Channel.

Interpolation of rates

You can use the tables in tidal stream atlases to refine the rates between neaps and springs. However, tidal streams are affected by many factors such as wind and atmospheric pressure, and interpolation 'by eye' is usually quite sufficient for most practical purposes. The most accurate assessment can be made by observing the actual stream as you pass a buoy, fishing marker or some other fixed object.

Remember that if your course passes through an area marked by more than one tidal diamond or falls between two tidal stream arrows, it is also necessary to estimate what the rate is likely to be in the area between these positions.

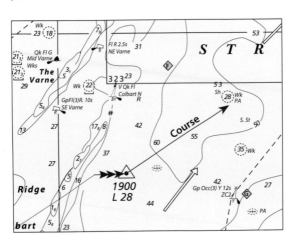

Coastal tidal streams

In a sailing yacht or other relatively slow vessel, the effects of tidal streams can be significant, and they should be carefully studied when planning a passage. In a yacht sailing at 5 knots, a 20NM trip you will take about 2 hours 50 minutes with a favourable 2 knot stream, but almost 4 hours longer (6 hours 40 minutes) if the same stream is against you.

Coastline Streams tend to run faster round headlands and through narrow channels, but slower offshore or in bays.

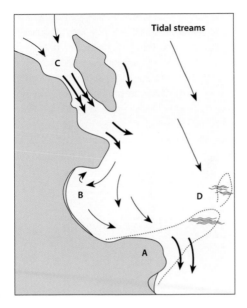

Sea bed Where an underwater ledge projects into a tidal stream, or anywhere else where there are abrupt changes in depths, broken water or overfalls may be encountered. These will usually be marked on the chart. A harbour entrance over a bar may pose no problem in a light wind and no stream, but can turn positively dangerous with a stiff onshore wind against a spring ebb.

Springs and neaps

Tides go up and down; tidal streams go to-and-fro.

Many factors – known as harmonic constituents – are taken into account when predicting the tides and producing tide tables. The gravitational forces of the moon and (to a lesser extent) the sun are the most significant. These cause a bulge of water to move round the globe as it rotates on its axis. When the moon and sun are both in line with the earth, their combined pull on the sea's surface is at its greatest, causing maximum rise and fall of the tide (*spring* tides); when they are at right angles to the Earth, tidal rise and fall is a minimum (*neap* tides).

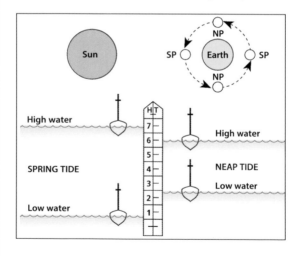

Spring tides occur roughly every fortnight, 2–3 days after full and new moons. Neap tides occur when the moon is in its first and last quarter. At any given place, spring high tide will always be at approximately the same time, and the corresponding low water about six hours later. At Dover, for example, high water springs is at about 0000 and 1200, whereas at Plymouth is at about 0600 and 1800. Thus, by simply observing the moon it is possible to estimate the *range* of the tide and the time of high and low water.

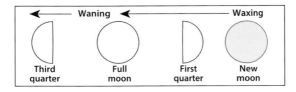

Range The difference between the heights of high and low water is the *range* of the tide.

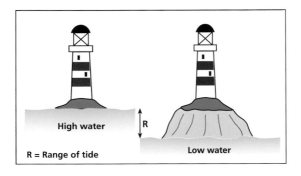

Tidal patterns

The depth of water, shape of the coastline and many other factors affect the tide, and no two places have exactly the same tidal pattern. To take an extreme example, the tidal range in the Bay of Fundy, Canada, can be 15 metres, while the Baltic and Mediterranean seas have almost no tide at all. In the UK, tides in the Bristol Channel can reach 14 metres, but at Portland the range may be less than 1 metre.

Around the British Isles and most of northwest Europe, the tides are *semi-diurnal*, having two high tides and two low tides each day, with the time between successive high waters being about 12 hours 25 minutes.

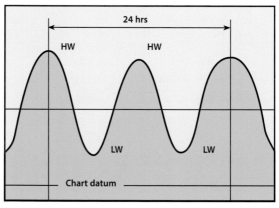

Semi-diurnal tide.

In the Pacific and around Australia, tides are *diurnal* with just one high and one low water each day.

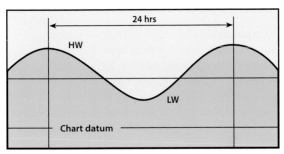

Diurnal tide.

Elsewhere, tides are *mixed*, having two high and low waters, but with the heights of the second tides each day varying greatly in height.

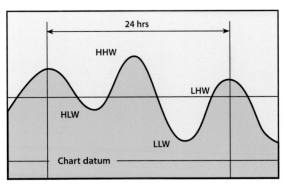

Mixed tide.

Chart datum

Chart datum (CD) is the level below which the tide rarely falls and from which the height of tide is measured.

Charted depths, as shown on charts, are referred to CD and thus represent the least depth, in metres, which may be encountered in that position. 5_3 indicates a charted depth of 5.3 metres.

Height of tide is the level of water above *chart datum*. The height of tide added to the charted depth gives the actual depth of water. A charted depth of 5_3 and a height of tide of 3_4 would therefore give a depth of 8_7.

The times and heights of high water (HW) and low water (LW) are given in tide tables, and can be found in almanacs, local publications and online. Most tidal apps show the heights and times of the tide for any selected time.

Tidal heights and chart datum

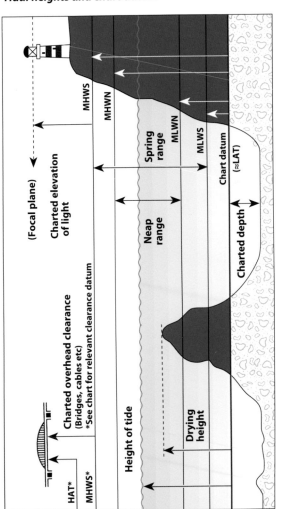

Focal plane

Charted elevation of light

Charted overhead clearance
(Bridges, cables etc)
*See chart for relevant clearance datum

HAT*

MHWS*

Height of tide

Drying height

MHWS

MHWN

MLWN

MLWS

Spring range

Neap range

Chart datum (≈LAT)

Charted depth

Drying heights

If a feature uncovers as the tide falls, the charted depth is underlined and the depth shown must be *subtracted* from the height of tide to find the actual depth. For example, a drying height of $\underline{5}_3$ and a height of tide of 7_6 would give a depth of 2_3.

The actual depth of water is obtained by an echo sounder or leadline. It is the charted depth plus the height of tide.

MHWS and MLWS *Mean High Water Springs* and *Mean Low Water Springs* are the average heights of tide at spring tides.

The charted elevations (heights) of lights are measured from MHWS.

MHWN and MLWN As above but for neap tides.

HAT and LAT *Highest Astronomical Tides* and *Lowest Astronomical Tides* are the highest/lowest levels which can be expected under average meteorological or any astronomical conditions except storm surges. Heights under bridges and cables are almost always given from HAT – but check the chart.

Finding the height of the tide

Tides do not rise and fall at a constant rate, but in most places they follow a sine curve with roughly the same shape either side of HW. However, the profile of the sea bed and coastline can affect the shape, causing irregularities which need to be taken into account when calculating the height of the tide for a particular time.

Tidal curves for *standard ports* can be found in tide tables and almanacs.

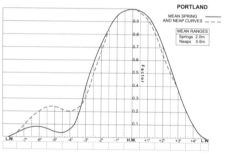

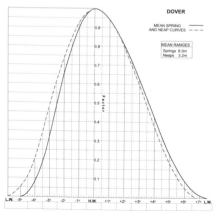

Standard/secondary ports

Standard ports have tidal characteristics observed over long periods, and may be used as a reference for other places which are usually, but not always, on the adjacent coast.

Secondary ports have similar tidal characteristics as a standard port but with some time and height differences. 'Secondary' applies only to the tides; it does not imply lesser importance.

Time zones

The relevant time zone is shown at the top of each tide table. For UK ports this will be Universal Time (UT) which is the same as Greenwich Mean Time (GMT). A correction must be made for daylight saving time (ie BST in the UK).

For timekeeping purposes, the world is divided into 24 Time Zones, each 15° of longitude wide. Zone 0 (7½°E to 7½°W) straddles the Greenwich Meridian. At sea, zones east of Greenwich (earlier in time) are labelled Zone –1 to –11; zones west of Greenwich (later in time) are labelled Zone +1 to +11. Be aware that some land-based charts may refer to time zones the other way round.

Universal Time (UT) is a datum to which broadcast times, times of sunrise/sunset, scientific data etc are referred. UT is also the name for the Standard Time (see below) usually kept in countries wholly or partly in Zone 0.

Standard Time, also called legal time, is the time kept in different countries but it is modified by Daylight Saving Time (eg BST) in the summer.

For all practical purposes, Greenwich Mean Time (GMT) is the same as UT.

 Note

Differences for secondary ports are related to the standard time of the standard port, so any adjustment for daylight saving must be made *after* applying the time difference.

Calculating tidal heights

For standard ports, the heights of HW and LW are taken from the tide tables and entered on a tidal graph. A line is then drawn from required time before or after HW to the appropriate curve (springs or neaps) and the height obtained from the graph.

On 1 May at Walton-on-the-Naze
a) What will the height of tide be at 1100 GMT?
and
b) At what time will the tide reach a height of 1.75m?

- First, mark up the graph with the Walton high and low water times and heights and join the heights with a line as shown.

- Now compare the predicted range of tide with the mean ranges at springs and neaps and decide which curve to use or whether to interpolate between them (see page 58).

To answer (a) Enter the graph at the required time – 1100 and proceed as shown by the **red** line to find the height of tide at this time: **2.9m approx**.

To answer (b) Enter the graph at the required height of 1.75m and proceed as shown by the **blue** line to find the time at which this height will occur: **0926 GMT approx**.

- The height found by graph when added to the depth shown on the chart is the actual depth at that place.

- A drying height shown on the chart when subtracted from the height found by graph will be the depth (if any) at that place.

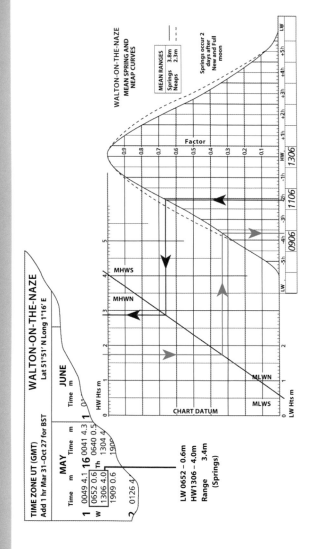

WALTON-ON-THE-NAZE
MEAN SPRING AND
NEAP CURVES

MEAN RANGES	
Springs	3.8m
Neaps	2.3m

Springs occur 2
days after
New and Full
moon

Factor

WALTON-ON-THE-NAZE
Lat 51°51' N Long 1°16' E

TIME ZONE UT (GMT)
Add 1 hr Mar 31–Oct 27 for BST

MAY		JUNE	
Time	m	Time	m
1 0049 4.1	**16** 0041 4.3	**1**
W 0652 0.6	Th 0640 0.5	
1306 4.0	1304 4.0	1909
1909 0.6		
2 0126 4		

LW 0652 – 0.6m
HW 1306 – 4.0m
Range   3.4m
(Springs)

MHWS
MHWN

HW Hts m

MLWN
MLWS

CHART DATUM

LW Hts m

LW   0906   1106   HW 1306

The differences for secondary ports are applied to the tide tables for their standard ports, then entered on the graph in the same way. Note that they differ according to the times of HW and LW at the standard port.

STANDARD PORT: WALTON-ON-THE NAZE							
TIMES				**HEIGHTS (Metres)**			
HW		LW		MHWS	MHWN	MLWN	MLWS
0000	0600	0500	1100				
AND	AND	AND	AND	4.2	3.4	1.1	0.4
1200	1800	1700	2300				
DIFFERENCES – BRADWELL							
+0035	+0023	+0047	+0004	+1.1	+0.8	+0.2	+0.1

Interpolation In the above example, the time difference for Bradwell is 35 minutes later when HW at Walton is at 0000 and 1200, and 23 minutes later when HW is at 0600 and 1800. For intermediate times, interpolation by eye will be adequate for most purposes. However, if greater accuracy is needed a graph may be drawn.

Interpolation - tidal differences

Example On a chosen day, HW Walton is 1405 3.8m. It can be seen that 1405 falls between the reference times of 1200 and 1800 on the table of differences (see above), therefore the exact difference which has to be applied lies proportionally between +35 to +23min (about +30min by eye).

To be more accurate
• Draw a graph as shown below with the Walton reference times 1200 to 1800 along one side and their corresponding differences for Bradwell +35 to +23min along the opposite side (see note on page 61).

- Close the triangle by drawing a line A–B between the last units on upper and lower lines.

- Enter the graph with HW Walton 1405 and draw a line **parallel to line A–B** to cut the lower line where the difference to be applied can now be read off (+31min).

The height of HW at Walton, 3.8, falls between 4.2 and 3.4m on the table of differences, which means that the difference to apply lies between 1.1 and 0.8m.

The precise difference could be found by constructing another graph with reference heights along one side and the corresponding differences along the other but in this instance, as the range of difference is so small (0.3m), interpolation by eye should be quite adequate.

Interpolation of differences

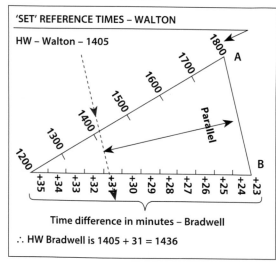

'SET' REFERENCE TIMES – WALTON

HW – Walton – 1405

1800 1700 1600 1500 1400 1300 1200 A

Parallel

B

Time difference in minutes – Bradwell

+35 +34 +33 +32 +31 +30 +29 +28 +27 +26 +25 +24 +23

∴ HW Bradwell is 1405 + 31 = 1436

The triangle may be drawn to *any* appropriate size and *any* suitable scale may be used, but it is **essential** to keep the reference times and their corresponding differences in the correct relationship as shown.

To determine intermediate heights, simply apply the times of HW and LW at the secondary port to the tidal curve for its standard port.

✳ Tip

Tidal height predictions for any given place are based upon the average height of tide recorded at that place over a long period of time. Usually these predictions are accurate but it is always best to allow a margin for error and/or the prevailing atmospheric and meteorological conditions whenever you are calculating clearance over an obstruction.

Rule of twelfths

This is a method of estimating the height of tide at any time between HW and LW. It assumes that the tidal curve is symmetrical and the duration of the rise and fall is six hours. The rule states that the tides rises (or falls):

$1/12$ of the range during the first hour
$2/12$ of the range during the second hour
$3/12$ of the range during the third hour
$3/12$ of the range during the fourth hour
$2/12$ of the range during the fifth hour
$1/12$ of the range during the sixth hour

However, the shape of the tidal curve is unlikely to be wholly symmetrical, and the tide is unlikely to rise and fall at the same rates. So this rule should only be used where very approximate values are acceptable.

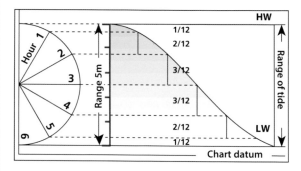

*The rise or fall of tide found by this rule must then be applied to the predicted height of high or low water as appropriate, to obtain the height of tide above chart datum.

South Coast anomalies

Because of the configuration of the coast between Swanage and Selsey, the times of LW are more easily defined than the times of HW. The tidal curves are therefore based on LW, but the method of finding intermediate heights are exactly the same as elsewhere.

As well as the springs and neaps curves, a third curve, based on the range of the tide at Portsmouth, is used for some of these ports. It is important to use the right one.

Find height of tide at Lymington at 2130 BST when at the standard port tidal predictions are:

   LW 1905 BST   – 1.1m
   HW 0204 BST   – 4.5m

1 Find the tidal data for Lymington by applying the differences to Portsmouth in the usual way.

2 Mark the corrected time and heights found onto the Lymington graph and join the heights with a line in the normal way.

3 Enter the graph at the time required (2130 BST), and proceed as shown by the red line to obtain the height of tide at this time.

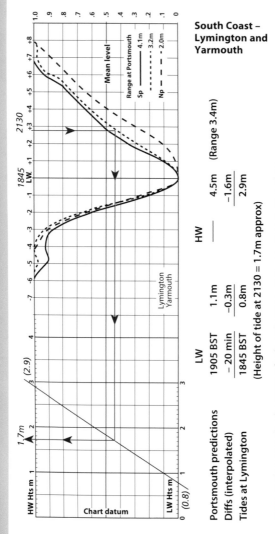

**South Coast –
Lymington and
Yarmouth**

	LW			HW	
Portsmouth predictions	1905 BST	1.1m		———	4.5m (Range 3.4m)
Diffs (interpolated)	– 20 min	–0.3m			–1.6m
Tides at Lymington	1845 BST	0.8m			2.9m

(Height of tide at 2130 = 1.7m approx)

Note: In this example, the range of tide at Portsmouth is very close to that of the critical curve so interpolation is between the critical curve and the spring curve.

Height of tide and depth of water

When a sounding is taken in tidal waters by leadline or echo sounder, it cannot be directly related to the charted depth until the height of tide has been established and subtracted from the reading.

This procedure is called reduction to soundings and may be used to check your estimated position (EP) or to assist in pilotage when running a line of soundings.

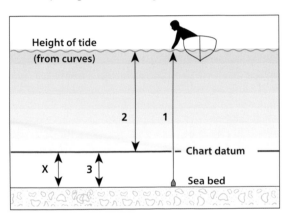

Height of tide (from curves)

2   1

Chart datum

X   3

Sea bed

Method

1	Take sounding
2	Subtract height of tide
3	Result is reduced sounding

When checking your EP, the reduced sounding (3) and the charted depth (X) should, ideally, agree.

Finding depths

Height of tide reduced to soundings using uncalibrated echo sounder

Most echo sounders can be adjusted to measure depth either from the waterline or from below the keel. If yours is calibrated to show the depth below the transducer, you will need to allow for this in your calculations. For this reason, it is simpler to adjust your echo sounder to read from the waterline.

1 Echo sounder reading	
2 Plus distance transducer to waterline	
3 Gives the actual depth	
4 Minus height of tide	
5 Gives the reduced sounding	

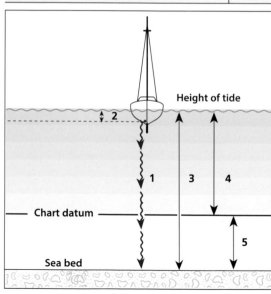

Finding depth to anchor

Will there be enough water at low water?
This is a quick and easy way of finding a safe depth in which to anchor.

Preparation
1 Find the times and heights of high and low water for the area you are in and plot the heights on your nearest standard port tidal curve as line **A**.

2 Mark on the LW line the minimum depth at which you want to be afloat (draught plus safety margin) and from this point draw a line **B** *parallel* to line **A**.

From now on line **A** is disregarded and anytime you want to anchor, the required depth can be read off quickly by reference to line **B**.

Example If HW at Walton is 3.5m at 1200 and LW is 0.8m at 1800, plot this on the curve as line **A**.

Now mark your minimum anchoring depth (say 2m) on the LW line and from it draw line **B** *parallel* to line **A**.

When you want to anchor, just check the time and draw a line up to the appropriate curve, across to line **B** then up or down to find the safest minimum depth to drop anchor. In this example, at 0920, your echo sounder needs to read at least 3.6m.

▶▶ Note
If your anchor cable is all chain you should veer 4 × max depth of water expected but if using rope with a chain leader, you should veer at least 6 × max depth of water expected.

Finding depth to anchor

Predictions:	HW 1200	3.5	Range 2.7
	LW 1800	0.8	
Time required:	0920		Min depth required: 2m

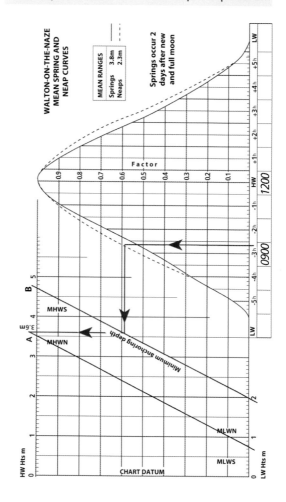

WALTON-ON-THE-NAZE
MEAN SPRING AND
NEAP CURVES

Springs occur 2
days after new
and full moon

MEAN RANGES	
Springs	3.8m
Neaps	2.3m

Factor

Minimum anchoring depth

MHWS
MHWN
MLWN
MLWS
CHART DATUM

HW Hts m
LW Hts m

Anchoring – depth by echo sounder

Finding depth by echo sounder to avoid going aground at LW

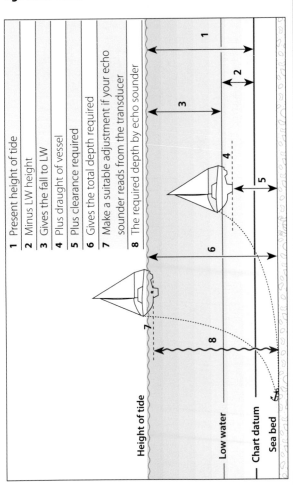

1 Present height of tide
2 Minus LW height
3 Gives the fall to LW
4 Plus draught of vessel
5 Plus clearance required
6 Gives the total depth required
7 Make a suitable adjustment if your echo sounder reads from the transducer
8 The required depth by echo sounder

Height of tide

Low water

Chart datum

Sea bed

Depth and clearance below the keel

To find clearance at LW using leadline

1	Depth by leadline	
2	Minus present height of tide	
3	Gives depth below chart datum	
4	Plus height of next LW	
5	Gives depth at LW	
6	Minus draught of vessel	
7	Gives clearance at LW	

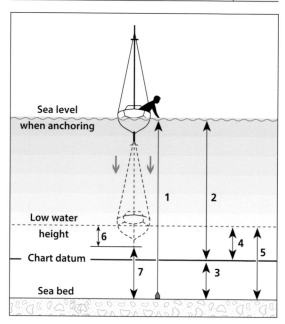

To find clearance at low water using echo sounder

1 Echo sounder reading	
2 Plus transducer to waterline (if necessary)	
3 Gives true depth of water	
4 Minus present height of tide	
5 Gives depth below chart datum	
6 Plus height of next LW	
7 Gives depth at LW	
8 Minus draught of vessel	
9 Gives clearance at LW	

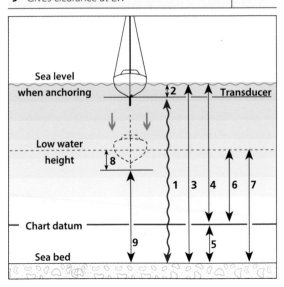

What is the depth beneath my keel?

1 Present height of tide	
2 Plus charted depth	
3 Gives total depth of water	
4 Minus draught of vessel	
5 Gives depth below the keel	

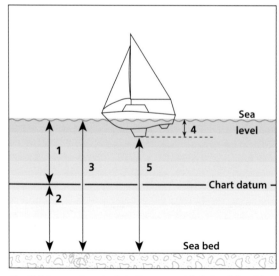

Use tidal curve to calculate the present height of the tide.

Height of tide required to clear a bank or bar

1 Draught of the vessel	
2 Plus clearance required	
3 Gives total depth required	
4 Minus charted depth	
5 Gives height of tide required	

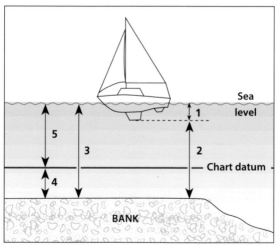

Use tidal curve to find the time at which height required will occur.

Height of tide required to clear a charted drying height

1 Draught of the vessel	
2 Plus clearance required	
3 Plus charted drying height	
4 Gives height of tide required	

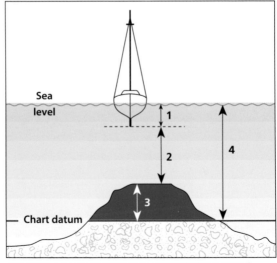

Use tidal curve to find the time at which the required height will occur.

Will my vessel clear a charted drying height?

1	Present height of tide	
2	Minus drying height	
3	Gives actual depth of water	
4	Minus draught of vessel	
5	Gives clearance beneath the keel	

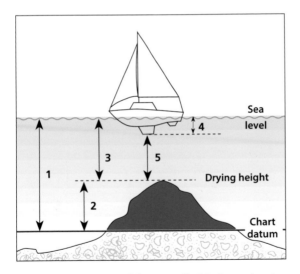

On a falling tide: *use tidal curve to find the latest time to cross in safety.*

On a rising tide: *use tidal curve to find the time at which the required height will occur.*

Clearances under bridges

The clearance under a bridge or cable that crosses a navigable waterway is clearly marked on large scale charts of an area. The clearance hitherto has been measured from the level of MHWS, but on many charts the vertical clearance is now measured from HAT.

The water level under a bridge will seldom be as high as this so the clearance is usually greater than that given. It should be remembered, however, that the water level in estuaries and rivers may be raised substantially by strong onshore winds, heavy rainfall, or by the relief of weirs upstream; for these reasons a good margin for error should be allowed.

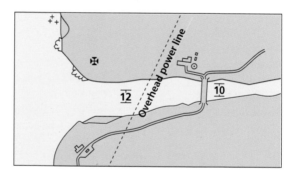

▶▶ Caution

When you have made certain that your mast or the boat's superstructure will clear the bridge, be sure to check that at the same time you also have enough water below your keel.

The difference between a *charted clearance* and the height of a vessel's mast (plus a suitable safety margin) is the fall of sea level below the given *clearance datum* (MHWS or HAT) that is needed to permit the vessel to pass under the bridge.

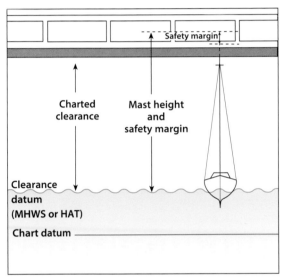

The appropriate clearance datum can be found on the chart.

✳ Tip

Whenever the height of your boat's mast or superstructure (plus safety margin) exceeds the charted clearance above the level of MHWS, you can use the tidal curves to find out when your boat will be able to pass under the bridge.

Tidal stream/current

In a flat calm sea with no current or tidal stream, the track on the chart will be the course to steer. This is rarely the case in practice. Even for the shortest passages it is good practice to calculate a course to steer; if you don't, it will almost certainly take longer to reach your destination or you may end up down tide and/or wind and face a tedious beat to get into harbour.

Tidal stream will have the greatest effect on the course to steer when it is on the beam. It will have no effect when from right ahead or right astern, although it will then affect your speed over the ground.

Current is a movement of water caused by factors other than the tides, usually meteorological and oceanographical. The combination of tidal stream and current is known as the **flow**. Currents are not as predictable as tidal streams but may need to be considered when calculating a course to steer.

Pressure on the sails drives a yacht forwards but also includes a sideways component. This is leeway and is measured as the difference, in degrees, between the boat's heading and her actual track through the water. In certain conditions, high-sided motor cruisers proceeding slowly in a rough sea may also make considerable leeway.

Calculating leeway is not an exact science and depends on wind strength, the point of sailing, hull and keel configuration, speed through the water and sea state. It might be possible to estimate leeway by comparing the angle made by the boat's wake and the actual heading, but in a lumpy sea this will be far from precise.

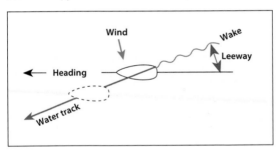

Leeway will be greatest when close-hauled and negligible when on a broad reach or running free. In most modern yachts it is unlikely to be more than 3–5° but may be greater in a stiff breeze and rough sea.

To apply leeway, simply steer towards the wind by the estimated number of degrees. If the wind is from your port side, steer to port; if the wind is from starboard, steer to starboard. Most helmsmen will tend to bias their course towards the wind anyhow, so may unwittingly compensate for any leeway.

Calculations

Calculating the course to steer – short passage

1. On the chart plot the track from your starting point (**A**) to your destination (**B**).

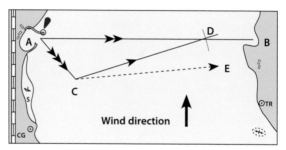

Wind direction

2. From **A** plot the predicted tidal stream vector during the passage (**A–C**). Use units of length equal to its rate in knots.

3. Draw an arc equal to your expected speed through the water from **C** to your track (**AB**). Where it cuts the track (which may be before or after **B**) is **D**.

4. The line from **C** to **D** is the initial course to steer, but this needs to be further refined by making allowances for variation and deviation (see pages 23–5).

Calculating the course to steer – long passage

Follow the steps 1–4 above, but at step 2 plot the tidal
stream vector for each hour of the passage in the position
you expect be at that time. Join the vectors together to
obtain the overall effect.

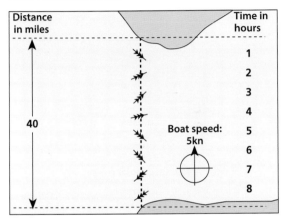

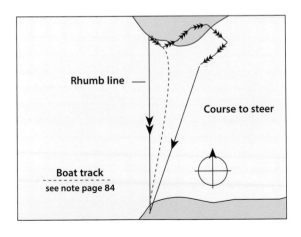

Rectilinear tidal streams

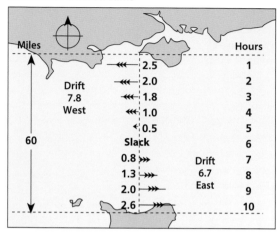

The movement of tidal streams for the period.

Distance ÷ **Estimated** = **Time to**
to go   **speed**   **cross**

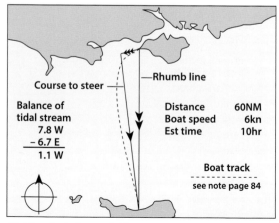

Course to steer

Rhumb line

Balance of
tidal stream
7.8 W
− 6.7 E
1.1 W

Distance	60NM
Boat speed	6kn
Est time	10hr

Boat track
- - - - - - - - -
see note page 84

Plotting the balance of tide.

If the stream runs in one direction during the flood then in the opposite direction during the ebb, such as for a typical cross-Channel crossing it is only necessary to add up the total set in each direction and subtract one from the other to determine the overall set.

Making allowance for the stream for each hour of the passage in order to follow the direct track on the chart is not efficient as you will sail a greater distance through the water. This may be necessary if there are hazards either side of the track, otherwise allow the boat to be set off track in each direction.

If you are lucky, you will arrive at your destination as planned. However, life is never that simple and you must monitor your progress carefully, making adjustments to the course as necessary.

Point of arrival

A prudent navigator will be mindful of the vagaries of tidal streams, currents and leeway, and aim to arrive up wind and/or up tide of the planned destination. How far depends on how accurately you can fix your position during the passage, the expected tidal stream in the final few hours, and the forecast wind speed and direction.

For instance, the ebb stream can be particularly strong between the Cherbourg peninsular and the north coast of Alderney, and if you get your calculations wrong you will probably wind up in Guernsey whether you like it or not. In this case, a point of arrival five miles up tide would not be unreasonable.

COURSE TO STEER

COURSE TO STEER

▶▶ Note

Steering a single course across an ebb and flood tide will take the boat well away from the required rhumb line but will be the shortest distance through the water. Check that no dangers exist on either side.

The alternative is to shape a separate course to steer for each hour of tidal stream. This will keep the boat on or close to the rhumb line but will not be as efficient as steering one course and allowing the boat to deviate from the rhumb line.

Destination to windward

When your destination lies directly up wind of the boat, it becomes necessary to beat towards it by sailing close-hauled on alternate tacks, preferably keeping within 10°–15° of the downwind line so as to be well placed to take advantage of any wind shifts as they occur.

Set off on the tack that points more directly towards your destination and work up to it with a series of relatively short tacks made between predetermined tack 'limiting lines', making due allowance for leeway and tidal stream in the usual way. Alternatively, if your objective is visible you can tack each time the appropriate bearing to either side of the direct line of approach is reached.

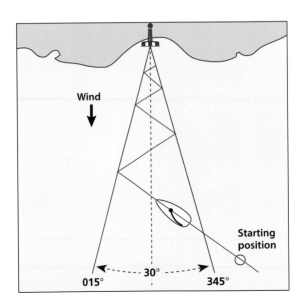

Lee-bowing the tide

If the tidal stream is expected to slacken or reverse direction, there is an advantage to be gained from holding the tack that puts the tide on the lee bow and letting it push the boat to windward. The freeing wind shift induced by the tide will also allow the boat to point higher on this tack, helping to get you towards your destination more quickly.

If the tidal stream is constant, however, there is no advantage to 'lee bowing' as you will lose whatever you have gained when you go onto the opposite tack.

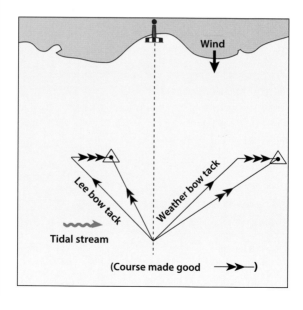

Estimated time of arrival

A very rough estimated time of arrival (ETA) can be found by simply dividing the distance by your expected overall speed over the ground. The Needles to Cherbourg is 60NM, so at 5.5 knots the passage will take about 11 hours.

You should adjust your departure time, if practicable, to make best use of any favourable stream. If the stream is directly astern or ahead just add or subtract the rate to or from your own speed. But if the stream is at an angle to your track, you will need to follow the same procedure as calculating the course to steer.

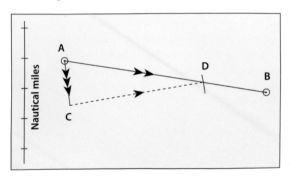

From your starting point **(A)** plot the tidal vector **(AC)** then use dividers to draw an arc on your track **(CD)** equal to your speed through the water. **AD** is the speed made good.

Estimating your time of arrival involves several approximate predictions (tidal rates, speed through the water etc) so be wary of giving your crew a 'precise' ETA. An early arrival will probably be popular, but you will get all the blame for arriving late.

Global Positioning System

The NAVSTAR Global Positioning System (GPS) consists of 24–31 satellites orbiting about 11,000 miles above the earth. Six satellites should be 'visible' at all times from anywhere on the earth's surface. Position accuracy can be less than 5 metres but may greater under certain circumstances. At sea around the UK, it is reasonable to assume an accuracy of about 10 metres.

Because the earth is not an exact sphere, mathematical models are used to establish horizontal datums for specifying position. GPS uses the World Geodetic System 84 (WGS84), and almost all official charts in NW Europe use this datum. Positions from a GPS receiver may, therefore, be plotted directly onto such charts without correction.

Some charts still use other datums, and it is essential to check what corrections are necessary before plotting your position. The datum and corrections will be shown on the chart.

Most GPS receivers and chart plotters can be programmed to include the relevant corrections, but it is only too easy to forget to switch to the correct datum when using different charts. Best to double check.

Waypoint navigation

A waypoint (WP) is simply a geographical position, on land or sea, which may be recorded in the log or stored electronically.

When establishing a WP it is very easy to enter lat and long coordinates incorrectly, so always check its position by a range and bearing from a known point. In the vicinity of the Greenwich meridian great care must be taken not confuse east and west.

Using waypoints

Self-evidently, any WP which you are going to pass through must be in safe water. You must also check that the direct route between two WPs does not lead you into danger; an intermediate WP may be necessary.

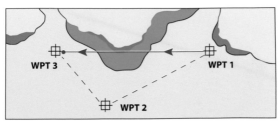

Be careful when you input a waypoint into a GPS, it is easy to enter a position incorrectly, or mistakenly plan a route that takes you into danger. Here, WPT 2 has been omitted from the plan in error. The incorrect route between WPT 1 and 3 could put you in dangerously shallow water.

Avoid using published WP lists. Other vessels may be using the same coordinates, thus increasing the risk of collision. Similarly, establishing a waypoint on a fixed object such as a buoy is not recommended. In poor visibility you may hit it!

Waypoint navigation

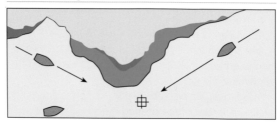

It is safer to plot a WPT near to a charted object rather than on top of it. Be aware that other boats may be using the same WPT.

If you are aiming for a WP, any tidal stream will mean that you have to continually adjust your course to keep heading for it. By doing so, you will sail further and may be set into dangerous waters. Always calculate a course to steer, and aim to keep the WP on a steady bearing.

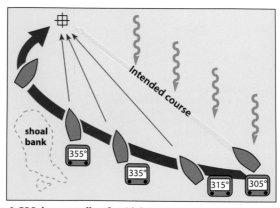

A GPS does not allow for tidal streams so always calculate the course to steer. If you repeatedly alter course to steer to a mark using bearings given by your GPS you will sail further and might put your boat in danger.

A 'web' of bearings and ranges from a WP can be used for rapid and accurate plotting on a chart without the need to use lat and long coordinates. Drawing a 'web' is a bit laborious but if you chose the position of the centre of a convenient compass rose on the chart as the WP, there is no need to draw a 'web' at all – just line up a straight edge on the reciprocal of the bearing of the WP as shown on GPS, and plot the distance using a pair of compasses.

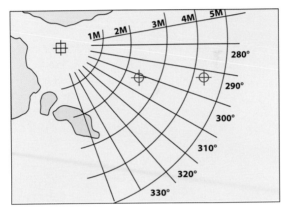

Traditional plotting methods can be difficult in high-speed boats. A web of ranges and bearings drawn on the chart from your arrival waypoint allows you to plot your position easily and quickly.

It is often quicker to plot your position using the GPS bearing and distance display than by taking co-ordinates from the latitude and longitude readout and transferring them onto the chart.

You needn't use just the waypoint you are aiming for to get a range and bearing. An alternative is to store the position at the centre of one of the chart's compass roses as a waypoint. You can then plot its range and bearing

Waypoint navigation

whenever you need to. You don't even need a plotter to do this. Any straight edge will do because it can be lined up directly on the compass rose itself, but do remember to read the bearing from the opposite side of the rose as the bearing is to the waypoint and then step off the distance from the centre of the rose – not the edge.

Variations of this can be used to keep within a certain distance off the planned track (cross track error (XTE)), or to keep with a 'cone' of bearings as you beat towards your destination. The bearings of the WP act as clearing bearings if dangers are close to your track.

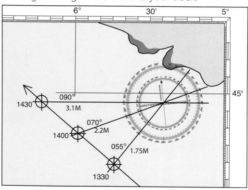

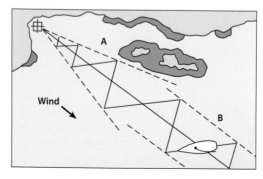

Chart plotters

All of the techniques above have been largely superseded by chart plotters. However, although you may have several independent GPS receivers on board (VHF radio, smartphone, tablet etc), a fixed chart plotter relies on power from the boat's batteries and its own dedicated GPS aerial. If either of these fail or are damaged – unlikely but not unknown – you must fall back on manual plotting.

That said, modern chart plotters are sophisticated and remarkably reliable. Many are multi-function displays (MFD) on which can be shown charts, GPS positions, tracks and routes, AIS, depth, speed through the water and more.

You must get to know your own chart plotter. Like most electronic devices, it probably has functions which you will never use, and those which you do need may not be entirely intuitive to access. Always have the user manual to hand.

There is a general misconception that electronic charts are more accurate than paper charts but, like their paper equivalents, they are only as accurate as the latest corrections. Downloading corrections may involve a wi-fi connection or an updated cartridge.

Passage planning apps

Passage planning apps are widely available and vary considerably in price and effectiveness. Some will produce a comprehensive plan which takes into account tidal streams and other variables; many are less sophisticated.

Whatever system you chose, if any, you must make yourself aware of its limitations. No app can make subjective decisions or be a substitute for experience and common sense. It would be very unwise to rely on a route generated by a passage planner without carefully checking that it allows sufficient clearances past hazards or over shoal water. When sailing, the wind, weather and sea state often dictate your course to steer; but most planning software will not take them into account.

That said, there are some excellent apps which are inexpensive and will produce the basis of a full-blown plan, saving much time and effort in the initial stages. You must then refine that plan to include such factors as the boat's capabilities, crew experience, the weather (present and forecast) and your own knowledge and experience.

Automatic Identification System

Class A/B

An automatic identification system (AIS) is compulsory in ships over 300 tons, but it is also widely fitted in yachts, motor cruisers and other small craft where its main purpose is to assist in collision avoidance. Unlike radar, which only gives a range and bearing of other contacts, AIS data includes identity, position, course and speed. With course and speed inputs from a receiving vessel, the closest point of approach (CPA) can also be displayed.

AIS data is transmitted via VHF, and the range is thus limited to 'line of sight' – about 10–20 miles depending on power output and the height of the aerial. There are three types of AIS:

Class A is fitted mainly in larger commercial vessels. Its power output is 12.5W.

Class B is designed for use in smaller craft. It is a simpler system than Class A, has a reduced power output (just 2W) and does not transmit as much information. Typical range of Class B is 5–10 miles.

Class B+ is more powerful than Class B and has many of the characteristics of Class A. It is more suited to larger, faster leisure craft and small commercial vessels which are not obliged to have Class A. Range is between Class A and 'basic' Class B.

Equipment

An AIS receiver requires GPS and VHF inputs. GPS is via a dedicated antenna or by connecting to a compatible chart plotter or computer (laptop, tablet etc). VHF signals are received using a separate VHF aerial or via a splitter, which allows both the VHF radio and the AIS receiver to share one aerial. The higher the aerial is mounted, the greater the range.

The simplest and cheapest way of receiving AIS data is via a suitably equipped **VHF radio**. This will allow other vessels' information to be displayed on the radio's screen. Some VHF radios include an **AIS transceiver** (receive and transmit). These save space but are significantly more expensive. One advantage of having a VHF radio which receives AIS is that you are able to select any vessel on the display and call her on DSC at the press of a button.

VHF radio with AIS (receive) function.

A **standalone AIS receiver** allows contacts and data to be displayed on its own screen or on a chart plotter or other suitable display. A separate aerial or a VHF splitter will also be required.

An **AIS transceiver** may be standalone, with its own display, or it may show data on another screen.

Connections may be by NMEA or USB. Some transceivers transmit data via wi-fi allowing contacts to be overlaid on electronic charts installed on, for example, a laptop or tablet. This allows you to use your device wirelessly anywhere in the boat while still having access to AIS data.

The great advantage of transmitting on AIS is that other vessels can detect you. This is particularly beneficial in restricted visibility.

AIS standalone transceiver.

Operation

Once set up, AIS is very simple to operate. Displays vary but will always show the positions of other vessels transmitting on AIS, and their identity, course and speed over the ground (COG and SOG) and closest point of approach (CPA). Heading, rate of turn and other information may also be available. Detection range and the screen range are adjustable.

Collision avoidance

AIS does not yet feature in the Colregs, and the Maritime and Coastguard Agency (MCA) advises that collision avoidance decisions should be based on visual and/or radar observations. One reason for this is that AIS provides courses and speeds *over the ground*, whereas Colregs compliance must be based on courses and speeds *through the water*. That said, AIS is undoubtedly a significant aid to collision avoidance.

Cautions

* Class A transmissions take priority over Class B, so in busy areas the latter may be excluded at times.
* Not all small vessels transmit on AIS, so a good visual and/or radar lookout is still essential.
* Some vessels may inadvertently transmit unreliable data.
* Some vessels (warships, for example) may not transmit at all for operational reasons.

Other uses

- Increasingly, buoys, lights and other aids to navigation (AtoN or A2N) are fitted with AIS. These are shown on Admiralty charts by a magenta circle round the A2N, and the notation 'AIS'.

- Virtual AIS (VAIS) is sometimes used where there is no physical mark. There is, for example, a VAIS about 3 miles north west of Cherbourg (in the same position as the old CH1 buoy).

- Vessel tracking systems and applications use AIS to display the positions of ships worldwide. *MarineTraffic* and *VesselFinder* are two examples. Basic data can be viewed free, while additional services incur a small charge.

As ever, the user manual for your installation should be read carefully to make best use of the available functions. Much more technical information on AIS can be found online.

AUTOMATIC IDENTIFICATION SYSTEM

Lights

Your distance from a charted feature provides a position line (actually, an arc) which can be useful in determining your position. Radar, if fitted, is an obvious 'range finder', but other methods are available.

The range at which you can first see a light above the horizon depends on your height of eye, the height of the light above sea level and its range. The height of a light is known as its *elevation* and is measured from mean high water springs (MHWS). It is shown on charts, in almanacs and other publications. For more accuracy, add the height of tide *below* MHWS to the charted elevation. This is rarely, if ever, needed for normal navigational purposes.

The range is the distance the light can be seen on a clear, dark night but this may be limited by the curvature of the earth. You will usually see the loom of a light before it pops over the horizon.

A table of distances is on page 210. Elevations are shown in the left-hand column, and height of eye is entered at the top. Similar tables can be found in *Reeds Nautical Almanac*.

If tables are not to hand, you can resort to mathematics. The formula is:

$$\sqrt{\text{Ht of eye (m)}} + \sqrt{\text{Ht of light (m)}} \times 2.075$$
$$\sqrt{\text{Ht of eye (ft)}} + \sqrt{\text{Ht of light (ft)}} \times 1.15$$
$$= \text{Distance off in nautical miles}$$

Vertical sextant angles

If you have a sextant onboard, you can use it to measure your distance from any charted object whose height is also charted. You need to be able to see the sea immediately below the object so in practical terms vertical sextant angles are usually limited to lighthouses.

▶▶ Note
The elevation of a lighthouse refers to the light itself, not the top of the structure.

Distance off by vertical sextant angle

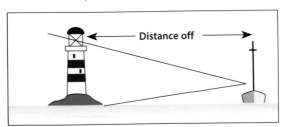

Vertical angle taken between the base of the lighthouse and FOCAL PLANE of the light, NOT the top of the lighthouse.

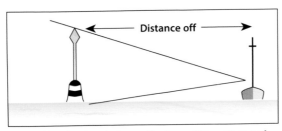

Vertical angle taken between the base of the object and its PEAK.

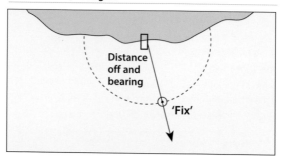

A bearing of the object and its distance off provide a 'fix'.

▶▶ Note

The height of an object on land is measured from the level of MHWS. If the sea level is below this datum when the sextant angle is taken, the apparent height of the object is increased, which also increases the angle being measured. This gives the impression that the boat is closer to the object than it actually is, and provides a slight safety margin. It should not be overlooked, however, that by the same reasoning, you will also be that much closer to any hazard that lies behind you.

Taking a vertical sextant angle on a lighthouse

Hold the sextant vertically, set the index to zero and view the centre of the light through the telescope. The true image will be seen through the plain half of the horizon glass and the reflected image in the mirror half.

Both images should coincide. Turn the micrometer drum so that the index bar moves along the arc away from you and the image will separate, the reflected image moving downward. Tilt the sextant to follow this movement until the centre of the light reaches the shore line. Read the angle and correct for index error.

Refer the corrected angle and the charted height of the light to the table on page 210 or to the appropriate table in the almanac to obtain a 'distance off'. Couple this with a bearing of the light taken at the same time as the sextant angle to obtain a 'fix' by bearing and distance.

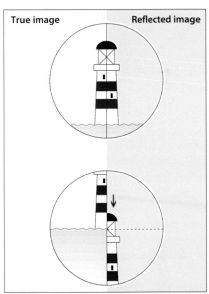

| True image | Reflected image |

▶▶ Note

If an almanac or tables are unavailable, the distance off by vertical sextant angle can be found by using the formula:

$$\text{Distance off (nm)} = \frac{1.852 \times \text{height in metres}}{\text{angle in minutes of arc}}$$

Astro navigation

Not many yachts now carry a sextant unless they are undertaking ocean passages. Even then, many skippers prefer to take several back-up GPS receivers rather than resorting to astro navigation. This is a pity because a sextant, an accurate timepiece and some simple tables are all you need to navigate offshore if all else fails. The *Reeds Astro Navigation Tables* provide all the data required along with clear instructions and some worked examples.

If your cruising is restricted to coastal sailing with the occasional offshore passage, a sextant can still be useful, as mentioned on page 101, but cost and a view that astro is a 'black art' deters most skippers from carrying one on board. However, sextants which are perfectly adequate for coastal work can be obtained for less than £300.

Any sextant must be carefully adjusted according to the manufacturer's instructions, and any residual error must be applied to subsequent readings. This is known as *index error*.

A brief description of the process for determining index error is below, but more detailed advice on the care, maintenance and use of sextants is beyond the scope of this book.

To find the index error

1 Clamp index bar and micrometer drum at zero.
2 Hold the sextant vertically and sight a clear, distant horizon, turning the drum until the true and reflected horizons form a single unbroken line.
3 The sextant reading indicates the index error.
4 If the reading is on the 'plus' side of zero it must be subtracted as a correction.
5 If the reading is on the negative side of zero it must be added.

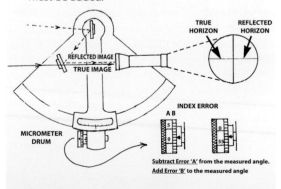

Subtract Error 'A' from the measured angle.
Add Error 'B' to the measured angle

Definitions

As a skipper you must have a thorough understanding of the *International Regulations for Preventing Collisions at Sea*, usually shortened to the *Collision Regulations* or simply the *Colregs*. They are mandatory, and you could be prosecuted you are involved in an incident at sea where it is found that you did not comply with the rules. They are reproduced in full in *Reeds Nautical Almanac* and many other publications dedicated to the subject.

What follows is a very brief summary of some of the rules. The definitions below are not necessarily the exact words used in the Colregs.

Vessel Any craft used or capable of being used as a means of transportation on water. This includes a yacht's rubber dinghy, whether under power or being rowed.

Power-driven vessel Any vessel being propelled by machinery. A yacht with her sails set but using her engine is, therefore, a power-driven vessel for the purposes of the Colregs.

Sailing vessel Any vessel under sail which is not using her engine for propulsion.

Fishing vessel A vessel engaged in fishing whose gear restricts her ability to manoeuvre. In practice, many fishing vessels seem to think they come under this definition even if their manoeuvrability is not restricted. They invariably show the relevant shapes at all times when underway. The best advice is to give them a wide berth.

Not under command (NUC) Vessels which, because of exceptional circumstances (eg mechanical breakdown), are unable to keep out of the way of other vessels. Not often encountered.

Restricted in ability to manoeuvre (RAM) As for NUC, but because of the nature of her work. This includes, but is not limited to, servicing navigation marks, conducting diving operations and dredging.

Constrained by draught A vessel which is severely restricted from deviating from her track because of the available depth of water.

Underway A vessel which is not at anchor or made fast to the shore (eg on a buoy) nor aground. Note that the term **making way** means that she is moving through the water. So it is quite possible to be underway but stopped.

Give-way vessel A vessel which is obliged to take action to avoid collision in accordance with the Colregs.

Stand-on vessel A vessel which is required to hold her course and speed in accordance with the Colregs. Note that under Rule 17 a stand-on vessel may take early action to avoid a close quarters situation or a collision if the give-way vessel does not appear to be obeying the Colregs.

No vessel ever has a 'right of way'. If, as the stand-on vessel, you find yourself in a situation where it becomes impossible for the give-way vessel alone to prevent a collision, you are obliged to take whatever action you deem necessary to avoid a collision.

Responsibilities between vessels

Overtaking Any vessel which is overtaking another is the give-way vessel and is obliged to keep clear. If a power-driven vessel is overtaking a yacht under sail, the former must keep clear and the yacht is obliged to hold her course and speed.

Common sense dictates (and so do the Colregs) that you must not get in the way of an overtaking vessel if she is constrained by her draught or following a narrow channel.

Sailing vessels must keep out of the way of:
- Fishing vessels.
- A vessel not under command.
- A vessel restricted in her ability to manoeuvre.

Power-driven vessels (including a yacht using her engine) must keep out of the way of:
- Sailing vessels.
- Fishing vessels.
- A vessel not under command.
- A vessel restricted in her ability to manoeuvre.

Common sense (Rule 2) says you should not follow the Colregs to the letter if common sense, sound seamanship and any special circumstances dictate otherwise. However, under normal circumstances the rules are obligatory.

Lookout (Rule 5) emphasises the necessity for keeping a good lookout.

Speed (Rule 6) You must adjust your speed to the prevailing conditions so that you can take appropriate action to avoid collision. A list of factors to be taken into account is shown in this rule.

Risk of collision (Rule 7) All vessels must determine if the risk of a collision exists. In a small craft, the best way of doing this is to take a series of visual bearings of the other vessel. If the bearing does not change significantly, you are heading for a collision.

Radar, if fitted, should also be used to determine the risk, but it is widely accepted that this is not always practicable in a small craft. However, it would be imprudent (and a contravention of Rule 7) if you did not use your radar in fog.

> **▶▶ Note**
> AIS can be a valuable aid to avoid collisions but it does not appear in the Colregs, nor is it recommended by the MCA for this purpose.

Avoiding collision (Rule 8)

The overarching requirements when giving way to another vessel are:

- You should make your intentions abundantly clear and take action in plenty of time.
- You should avoid passing close ahead of another vessel.
- An alteration of course to port (when under power) is rarely prudent when giving way.

When **under power** you are the give-way vessel:

- If approaching another vessel head-on or nearly head-on. In this case *both* vessels should take avoiding action.

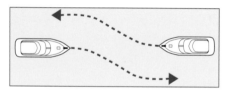

- If another power-driven vessel is closing on a steady bearing from your starboard side – unless she is overtaking.

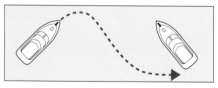

When **sailing** you are the give-way vessel:

- If you are on the port tack and the other is on starboard.

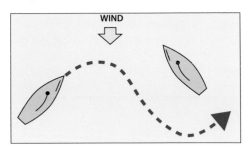

- If you are to windward of the other and you are both on the same tack.

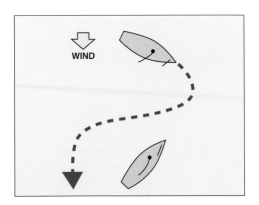

Narrow channels (Rule 9)

Common sense and judgment are required when navigating in a narrow channel. What may be relatively open water to a sailing yacht may be very restricting to a large ship. Generally, if the channel is marked with buoys, it is probably a narrow channel for the purposes of the Colregs.

If in any doubt, keep well clear of large ships in restricted waters.

Traffic separation schemes (Rule 10)

Sailing vessels and any craft under 20m LOA must not impede a power-driven vessel following a traffic separation scheme.

When crossing a traffic separation scheme you must do so on a *heading* which is at right angles to the general traffic flow. This is to ensure that you cross as quickly as possible.

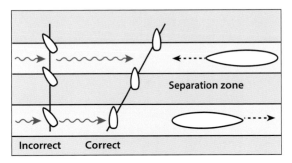

If sailing slowly, consider using the engine to get across.

Restricted visibility (fog) (Rule 19)

Rule 19 is much misunderstood. It applies to vessels which are not in sight of one another when navigating in *or near* an area of restricted visibility. This usually means fog but may be heavy rain, snow etc.

The actions required to avoid collision in fog are quite different from those when you can see the other vessel:

- You *must* sound the appropriate sound signals.
- If you detect a vessel on radar, you *must* determine if a risk of a close quarters situation exists. Unless you are *sure* that it doesn't, you must take avoiding action.
- *Do not alter course to port* for a vessel ahead of the beam (unless overtaking);
- *Do not alter course towards* another vessel which is on the beam or abaft the beam. In practice, this means that you should alter course to *starboard* for all vessels *except* for those on your starboard quarter or if you are overtaking. Whatever you do, you must also keep tracking the other vessel until all risk is over.
- If you hear a fog signal forward of the beam but can't be sure that no risk exists, you must reduce your speed, or even stop, until the situation clarifies.

Any device which is capable of producing long and short blasts may be used. A referee's whistle is particularly effective; aerosol horns can run out of gas.

Long blast (—) = 4–6 seconds

Short blast (●) = About 1 second

Sound signals in fog

Sounded at least every 2 minutes:

——	Power-driven vessel making way through the water
——●●	Sailing vessel making way through the water
—— ——	Any vessel underway but stopped in the water
——●●	Restricted in ability to manoeuvre (RAM) Restrained by draught Not under command (NUC) Fishing Towing
——●●●	Vessel being towed (if manned)

Manoeuvring signals

+ Turning to starboard   ●
+ Turning to port   ●●
+ Engines going astern   ●●●
+ If unsure of another vessel's intentions   ●●●●●

Signals in narrow channels

+ Approaching a blind bend   —
+ Intend to overtake to starboard   — — ●
+ Intend to overtake to port   — — ●●
+ Agreement by vessel being overtaken   — ● — ●

Signals at anchor or aground (in restricted visibility)

Small craft under 12m LOA are not obliged to sound the following signals but must make some other efficient sound signal at least every 2 minutes.

To be sounded at least every minute:

+ Vessels less than 100m LOA   Bell for 5 seconds
+ Vessels more than 100m LOA   Bell (5s) forward; gong (5s) aft
+ All vessels (optional warning if required)   ● — ●

Aground: same signals as at anchor but preceded and followed by 3 strokes of a bell.

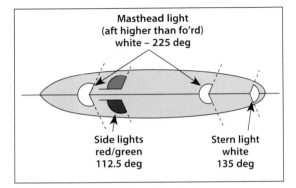

Masthead light
(aft higher than fo'rd)
white – 225 deg

Side lights
red/green
112.5 deg

Stern light
white
135 deg

All-round light Shows an unbroken light over 360°.

Masthead light Shows a white light from 22.5° abaft the beam through right ahead to 22.5° abaft the beam on the other side.

Side light Shows from 22.5° abaft the beam to right ahead. Red to port, green to starboard.

Stern light (aka overtaking light) Shows from 22.5° abaft the beam through right astern to 22.5° abaft the beam on the other side.

Towing light Same as stern light but yellow. Mounted above the stern light.

▶▶ Note
There are 32 points of the compass in 360°. Each point is therefore 11.25°, so 22.5° (as above) is 2 points.

Lights

Lights for sailing vessels under 20m LOA

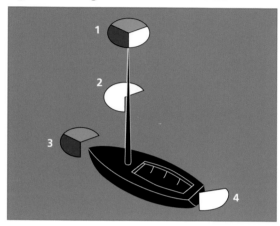

- Side lights (3). May be separate lanterns or combined into one lantern at the bows.
- Stern light (4).

These lights may be combined in a single tri-colour lantern at the masthead (1).

Lights for sailing vessels under power

- Side lights and stern light (as above) but *must not* show the optional tri-colour light.
- Streaming light (2). Does not have to be at the top of the mast.

Lights for sailing vessels under 7m LOA

- As above if possible. If not, **must** have a white light ready to show to avoid collision.

Lights for power-driven vessel

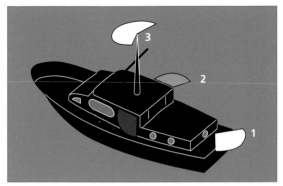

Vessels 12 to 20m LOA

- Side lights (may be combined) (2).
- Masthead light, at least 2.5m above the side lights (3).
- Stern light (1).

Vessels under 12m LOA

- As above. Masthead light must be at least 1m above the side lights.
- Masthead and stern lights may be combined into one all-round light at or near the masthead.

Vessels under 7m LOA and max speed 7 knots

- Side lights if practicable. Otherwise, all-round white light (or a torch).

All vessels at anchor

- All-round white light where it can best be seen.

☀ Tip

An anchor light at the masthead in a yacht may not be readily seen by other yachts. Better to show it near eye level: 3–4m above the waterline. A battery-powered lantern is a good option.

Larger vessels

Vessels **over 50m LOA** must show two all-round lights, one forward and one aft. The forward light must be higher than the after light.

Vessels **over 100m LOA** must also illuminate their decks.

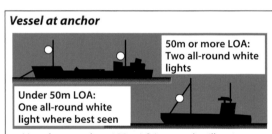

Vessel at anchor

50m or more LOA: Two all-round white lights

Under 50m LOA: One all-round white light where best seen

- Vessels more than 100m LOA must also illuminate their decks.

By day Shows a black ball.

Lights and daymarks on vessels

Vessels towing

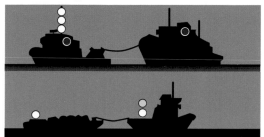

♦ Two masthead lights forward in a vertical line or if the length of tow exceeds 200m – three lights in a vertical line. Also side lights, stern light and a yellow light mounted above the stern light.

Vessel being towed

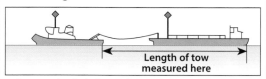

Length of tow measured here

♦ Stern and side lights only.

By day When length of tow is over 200m both vessels display a diamond shape.

Vessel constrained by draught

- Three all-round red lights with normal navigation lights when making way.

By day Shows a black cylinder.

Vessel not under command (unable to comply with the rules)

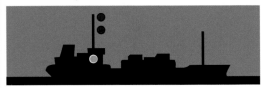

- Two all-round red lights and when making way – stern and side lights. (Not a distress signal.)

By day Shows two black balls in a vertical line.

Vessel aground

- Two all-round red lights and anchor lights. (Not a distress signal.)

By day Shows three black balls in a vertical line.

Vessels trawling

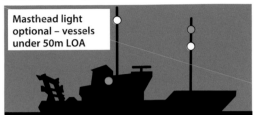

Masthead light optional – vessels under 50m LOA

- Two all-round lights green over white and lights for a power-driven vessel making way.

Pair trawling

- Vessels trawling as a pair direct searchlights forward and towards one another.

Vessel fishing (other than trawling)

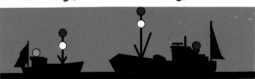

- Two all-round lights red over white, plus stern and side lights when making way.

By day Fishing or trawling: two cones apex together.

Additional signals – Vessels fishing in close proximity
Trawler hauling nets: ⚪   Shooting nets: ⚪
Two all-round lights ⚫   *Two all-round lights* ⚪
Vessel using purse seine gear: ✴
Alternate flashing yellow ⚪

Lights

Vessels restricted in their ability to manoeuvre

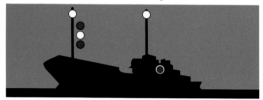

- Three all-round lights – red/white/red in a vertical line and masthead – stern and side lights when making way.

By day Shows a black ball over a diamond over a ball.

Vessels engaged in underwater operations or dredging

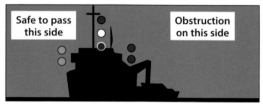

Safe to pass this side

Obstruction on this side

- Two red lights in a vertical line on the 'foul side' and two green lights on the unobstructed side.
- When making way, also shows masthead, stern and side lights. If anchored does **not** show anchor lights.

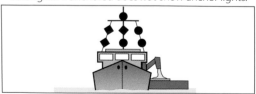

By day The red lights would be replaced by black balls and the green lights by black diamond shapes.

Vessels minesweeping

- Three all-round green lights with normal navigation lights.

By day All-round green lights are replaced by black balls.

* **It is dangerous to approach closer than 1000m astern or 500m on either side of this vessel.**

Pilot vessel: on duty

- Two all-round lights white over red and stern and side lights when making way. At anchor shows an anchor light.

By day Flies a white and red flag.

Hovercraft and hydrofoils

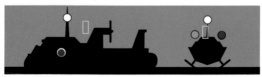

- Normal lights for power-driven vessels and an all-round flashing yellow light when in nondisplacement mode.

COLLISION REGULATIONS

Regulations

There are only a few regulations in Safety Of Life At Sea (SOLAS) which affect leisure craft. Chapter V lists those measures which *must* be complied with, whatever the size of your vessel.

Radar reflector All vessels must carry a radar reflector if practicable. Ideally, it should be permanently hoisted as high as possible.

Life-saving Signals An illustrated copy of the life saving signals must be carried on board, and be readily available. They are reproduced in this book (pages 135–6) and also in *Reeds Nautical Almanac*. The SOLAS requirement would be met if either of these is carried.

Danger messages Every skipper has a duty to report to the Coastguard anything which is a serious hazard to navigation, and which has not already been reported. An example would be a sighting of a semi-submerged container.

Distress messages You must respond to distress signals at sea, and assist as best you can. However, if you are not in a position to help there is no need to respond.

You must not use any distress signal unless you have a genuine emergency.

Passage planning You should plan *any* passage, and SOLAS V *requires* you to plan a passage which takes you out of sheltered waters. For this purpose, 'sheltered waters' are areas where the significant wave height cannot be expected to exceed 2.0 metres at any time.

126

A record of your plan is not mandatory but, if you are involved in an incident at sea, you may find it hard to prove that you made one if you don't write it down.

The following should be considered in a passage plan:

+ **Weather** Check the weather forecast before departure, and note what forecasts are available while on passage.

+ **Navigation** Consult relevant publications – charts, almanacs, pilot books etc – and be aware of navigational hazards. Plan your route accordingly.

+ **Tides** Check the times and heights of high and low water, make good use of tidal streams and be aware of any tidal 'gates'.

+ **Limitations of your vessel** Your boat should be suitable and appropriately equipped for the intended passage. This includes safety gear and sufficient fuel, water and food.

+ **Crew** Be sure your crew have sufficient expertise and strength to undertake the passage. Consider how they would cope if you are incapacitated by illness or accident.

+ **Contingency plan** Tell someone ashore about your plans and what actions they should take if you are overdue.

> ▶▶ **Note**
> Identify any harbours where you can find shelter or take refuge if things go wrong.

Calling for help

VHF radio is the primary means of calling for help in an emergency. Your options are:

* **Voice call** Normally on VHF Ch16, using either the format for Distress (MAYDAY) or for Urgency (PAN PAN).

1 **Mayday – Mayday – Mayday**
2 **This is** – Name of vessel three times
3 **Mayday** – Name of vessel once
4 **Give your position**
5 **State the nature of the emergency**
6 **Type of assistance required**
7 **Give any other helpful information**
8 **Over** – end of message

1 **PanPan** – PanPan – PanPan
2 **All stations** – All stations – All stations
3 **This is** – Name of vessel three times
4 **Give your position**
5 **State the nature of the problem**
6 **Type of assistance required**
7 **Over** – end of message

Note: A Distress alert must *only* be sent if you or your vessel is in **grave and imminent danger**.

* **DSC Call** Use the DSC Distress button on the radio. Read the user manual to acquaint yourself with the procedures on your particular radio.
* **EPIRB/PLB** Activate an Emergency Position Indicating

Radio Beacon (EPIRB) or Personal Locator Beacon (PLB). If possible, always send a Distress alert as well.

Flares are now generally considered to be a secondary means of alerting others to your predicament. However, they can be useful for pinpointing your position to rescue assets (lifeboats, helicopters etc).

- **Red parachute flares** can be seen for up to 25 miles in clear conditions, but only burn for a few seconds. Always send up a second flare soon after the first has burnt out to allay any doubts. *Never* fire towards a helicopter.

- **Hand-held red flares** have a limited range but may be useful inshore or when other vessels are nearby. Beware – they get very hot.

- **Orange smoke** may be used to pinpoint your position and to indicate the wind direction to a helicopter.

- **LED flares**. Pyrotechnic flares are potentially dangerous. LED 'flares', which have a long battery life and transmit very bright SOS signals, are available and worth considering as an alternative.

> ▶▶ **Note**
> More information on the use of VHF radio, including a full description of Distress and Urgency procedures, and the Global Maritime Distress and Safety System (GMDSS) may be found in the *Reeds VHF Handbook*, also published by Adlard Coles Nautical.

Personal safety

The skipper has total responsibility for the safety of the crew. He or she should hold a safety brief before sailing to include:

- Use of the lifesaving gear.
- Precautions to be taken to prevent falling overboard.
- Suitable clothing.
- Rules for the wearing of harnesses and lifejackets.
- Location of fire extinguishers and basic firefighting.

The length and depth of the brief will depend on the experience of the crew and their familiarity with the boat.

Clothing Inexperienced crew may not appreciate how cold it can be when out at sea. They should be encouraged to put on more layers than they think is necessary. It is much easier to remove some clothes than to put on more.

The temperature of the sea is a significant factor. At less than 10°C an unprotected person in the water could lose consciousness in 30 minutes; survival time is less than 4 hours.

Lifejackets There must be a suitable, well-fitting lifejacket on board for every crew member, and everyone must know how to fit and inflate it. The chances of successfully recovering a 'man overboard' (MOB) are thus significantly increased. Most skippers will insist that lifejackets are worn on deck:

- At all times when underway by non-swimmers.
- In rough seas and/or strong winds. Nasty tidal overfalls can occur even in windless conditions.
- At night.
- In fog.
- In the dinghy, except in very sheltered waters.

Harnesses A lifejacket will not prevent you from falling overboard.

If sailing two-handed, it is almost impossible to recover an unconscious or exhausted MOB except, perhaps, in a flat calm. A safety line attached to either a lifejacket or a dedicated harness will greatly help to keep you safely on board. The other end must, of course, also be attached to a strong point or jackstay, *not* the guardrails.

You may decide that the chances of being run down in fog outweigh the benefit of wearing a harness; you don't want to be dragged down with the boat.

Liferaft In sheltered inshore waters, a liferaft may be unnecessary if help is close to hand. But it would be very unwise to sail offshore without a liferaft which is designed for the maximum number of crew likely to be on board.

If it is stowed on deck or on the pushpit, you must be able to deploy it swiftly by some sort of quick-release mechanism.

A valise liferaft should be stowed out of the weather, so you need to plan how to get it on deck and into the water as fast as possible.

Make sure any liferaft is serviced in accordance with the manufacturer's recommendations.

Abandon ship

This is a last resort as it has been shown that the chances of survival are greatly increased if you stay on board unless the boat is actually sinking or has a fire which can't be contained.

If you do abandon ship, the aim is to step into the liferaft without getting wet. If time permits, collect warm clothing, water and food, and anything which will assist in your rescue.

Examples include:
◆ Hand-held VHF radio
◆ GPS receiver
◆ Flares
◆ PLBs.

Before launching the liferaft, secure the painter (which activates inflation) to a strong point in the boat. Once it is fully inflated send the strongest and heaviest crew member into the raft to stabilise it and to help the others to get in.

Helicopter rescue

For more details, see the 'Safety' chapter in *Reeds Nautical Almanac*.

* If necessary, use hand-held flares or orange smoke to pinpoint your position.
* Once VHF contact has been made, follow *precisely* the instructions given by the helicopter crew. When the helicopter is overhead, it will probably be too noisy to hear your radio.
* If you are able to make way, it is likely that you will be asked to steer a course with the wind about 30° on your port bow. This allows the pilot, who sits in the right-hand seat, to see you while flying into the wind.
* A weighted line will be lowered first. Allow it to touch the boat or the water to discharge any static electricity before handling it. *Do not* make it secure to the boat.
* The winchman will then be lowered to you. Do exactly what he says!

Search and Rescue Unit Replies
You have been seen, assistance will be given as soon as possible.

OR

Orange smoke flare.

Three white star signals or three light and sound rockets fired at approximately one-minute intervals.

Surface to Air Signals

Message	International Code of Signals			ICAO/IMO Visual Signals
Require assistance	V	✕	··· —	V
Require medical assistance	W	▣	· — —	X
No or negative	N	▦	— ·	N
Yes or affirmative	C	▤	— · — ·	Y
Proceeding in this direction				↑

Note: Use International Code of Signals by means of lights or flags or by laying out the symbol on the deck or ground with items that contrast highly with the background.

Air to Surface Direction Signals
Sequence of three manoeuvres meaning proceed to this direction.

1

Circle vessel at least once.

2

Cross low, ahead of vessel rocking wings.

3

Overfly vessel and head in required direction.

Your assistance is no longer required.

Cross low, astern of vessel rocking wings.

Note: As a non-preferred alternative to rocking wings, varying engine tone or volume may be used.

135

Life-saving signals

Shore to Ship Signals
Safe to land here.

OR

K

Vertical waving of both arms, white flag, light or flare.

Morse code signal by light or sound.

Landing here is dangerous. Additional signals mean safer landing in direction indicated.

 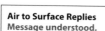

OR

S: •••
Morse code signals by light or sound.
R: •—•
Land to the right of your current heading
L: •—••
Land to the left of your current heading.

Horizontal waving of white flag, light or flare. Putting one flag, light or flare on ground and moving off with a second indicates direction of safer landing.

Air to Surface Replies
Message understood.

 OR OR

OR

T **R**

Drop a message.   Rocking wings.   Flashing landing or navigation lights on and off twice.

Morse code signal by light.

Message not understood – repeat.

 OR

OR

•—•   •——•   —
R   **P**   **T**

Straight and level flight.   Circling.

Morse code signal by light.

Surface to Air Replies
Message understood – I will comply.

OR

—
T

OR

Change course to required direction.

Morse code signal by light.

Code & answering pendant 'Close Up

I am unable to comply.

Note: Use the signal most appropriate to prevailing conditions.

—•
N

OR

International Flag 'N

If sensible precautions are taken, the risk of falling over the side should be negligible. But it does happen, so you must have a well-understood, and practised, plan for an MOB recovery.

'One hand for the ship; the other for yourself' is excellent advice but may not be enough. A well-fitting harness – which may be integrated with a lifejacket – and a safety line with self-locking clips on both ends is essential for all members of the crew.

The boat should have strategically placed strong points which can be reached by crew when coming up from below and which can be used by everyone in the cockpit without getting tangled up.

On deck, webbing jackstays anchored securely forward and aft, and run outside the standing rigging, will enable you to clip on in the cockpit and have a free run to the bows. The exact layout will depend on the boat and your preferences.

Never clip on to running rigging or the guardrails. The former may be released without warning; the latter are not designed for the considerable forces imposed by a person falling overboard.

Immediate actions

Three actions should be taken simultaneously:

* Shout **'Man overboard!'**. Do this even if it is obvious to everyone else; it is the trigger for all that follows.

* **Deploy lifebelts**, danbuoys and any other relevant MOB recovery equipment.

* **Tell someone to keep their eyes on the MOB**, *and do nothing else*. This action is the most important. It is very easy to lose sight of someone in the water, especially in choppy conditions. If visual contact is lost, it will be even harder to find the person again. The quicker you can get the casualty back on board, the better the chances of a successful outcome. The two greatest risks are losing sight of the MOB and the onset of hypothermia. Both of these risks can be minimised by keeping close to the MOB.

* Unless the sea is flat calm, put out a **distress alert**, either by DSC or by voice. If in doubt, do it anyway. However, the previous actions should take priority as they all help to keep in contact with the MOB.

There are many ways to manoeuvre to recover an MOB, but by far the simplest is to crash tack so the boat is hoveto. This works for any point of sailing.

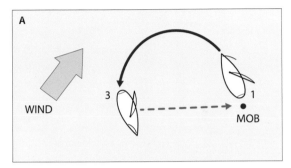

A – Sailing close-hauled or on a beam reach.

1 Tack *immediately* but without touching the genoa sheet.

2 You will then be hove-to upwind of the MOB. See note below.

B – Running downwind or on a broad reach

1 Turn *immediately* towards the wind, hauling in both mainsail and genoa.

2 Hold your course for a few moments before continuing through the wind but without touching the genoa sheet.

3 You will then be hove-to upwind of the MOB. See note on page 140.

Manoeuvring under sail

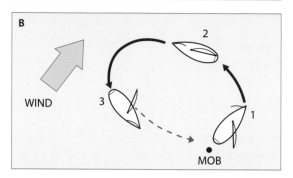

▶▶ Note

1 In both cases make the initial turn as quickly as possible to remain close to the MOB. If you lose sight of the casualty, the chances of recovery are severely reduced.

2 Be prepared to start the engine for better control in the final stages.

3 Consider dropping/furling both sails – but don't lose sight of the MOB.

Manoeuvring under power

The same principles hold true: keep the casualty in sight, and get back to him/her as quickly as possible.

In calm conditions where the is little risk of losing visual contact, just put the helm hard over (turning into the wind is quicker than turning downwind) and manoeuvre to a position just up wind of the MOB.

If there is a risk of losing sight of the MOB, a **'Williamson turn'** will get you to a position where you are on a reciprocal course and heading down your original track – where you should spot the casualty.

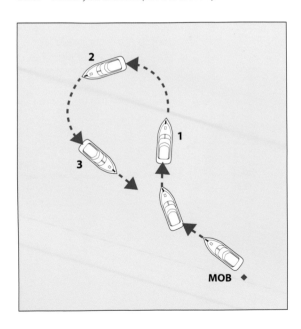

Manoeuvring under power

* Put the helm hard over to *starboard* until you have added about 50° to your heading (the angle will vary from boat to boat).
* Put the helm hard over to *port* and continue the turn until you are heading down the original track towards the MOB.

▶▶ Note

The reason for making the initial turn to starboard is that most people find it easier to add to the course than subtract. From a manoeuvring point of view, it makes no difference which way you turn.

VHF radio

VHF radio is the principal means of communicating at sea, although the Morse code still has its uses, as do signalling flags. You should at least make yourself familiar with some of the more common codes and signals, even if you don't commit them to memory. However, any word you spell over the radio must be done using the phonetic alphabet, and you should be able to do so without any hesitation.

Detailed guidance on the operation of VHF radio and associated voice procedures may be found in the *Reeds VHF Handbook*.

Some prowords used in radio transmissions can cause confusion:

This is   Indicates who is calling (*This is yacht* …).

Received   I have received and understood your message.
(**Roger** is still frequently used. It is not strictly correct but an acceptable alternative).

Over   I have finished transmitting and await your reply.

Out   I have finished transmitting and do not expect a reply.
(*Note*: *Never* say 'Over and out'. It makes no sense.)

Say again   Repeat your message or part of the message (*Say again your ETA*).

I say again In response to above (*I say again, my ETA is 1245.*)

I spell Used to confirm a word. Always use the phonetic alphabet.

Station calling When you are not sure of the name of the calling station (*Station calling yacht ..., say again your name*).

Correction (*My ETA is 1145. Correction: 1245.*)

- To operate the radio you must hold a Short Range Certificate (SRC). To obtain it you need to attend an RYA course and pass a short test.
- All radio equipment on board, including radar, AIS and EPIRBs/PLBs must be shown on the Ship Radio Licence issued by Ofcom.

  Both of the above are legal requirements.

A	ALPHA	▪ ━	N	NOVEMBER	━ ▪
B	BRAVO	━ ▪ ▪ ▪	O	OSCAR	━ ━ ━
C	CHARLIE	━ ▪ ━ ▪	P	PAPA	▪ ━ ━ ▪
D	DELTA	━ ▪ ▪	Q	QUEBEC	━ ━ ▪ ━
E	ECHO	▪	R	ROMEO	▪ ━ ▪
F	FOXTROT	▪ ▪ ━ ▪	S	SIERRA	▪ ▪ ▪
G	GOLF	━ ━ ▪	T	TANGO	━
H	HOTEL	▪ ▪ ▪ ▪	U	UNIFORM	▪ ▪ ━
I	INDIA	▪ ▪	V	VICTOR	▪ ▪ ▪ ━
J	JULIETT	▪ ━ ━ ━	W	WHISKEY	▪ ━ ━
K	KILO	━ ▪ ━	X	X-RAY	━ ▪ ▪ ━
L	LIMA	▪ ━ ▪ ▪	Y	YANKEE	━ ▪ ━ ━
M	MIKE	━ ━	Z	ZULU	━ ━ ▪ ▪

Numbers and Morse

0	ZERO	━ ━ ━ ━ ━	5	FIFE	▪ ▪ ▪ ▪ ▪
1	WUN	▪ ━ ━ ━ ━	6	SIX	━ ▪ ▪ ▪ ▪
2	TOO	▪ ▪ ━ ━ ━	7	SEV-EN	━ ━ ▪ ▪ ▪
3	TREE	▪ ▪ ▪ ━ ━	8	AIT	━ ━ ━ ▪ ▪
4	FOW-ER	▪ ▪ ▪ ▪ ━	9	NIN-ER	━ ━ ━ ━ ▪

Morse code is no longer routinely used to send messages but it should not be neglected by the sailor because S O S ▪ ▪ ▪ ━ ━ ━ ▪ ▪ ▪ by Morse is internationally recognised as a distress signal and, of course, many charted buoys and beacons have lights with Morse characteristics, ie:

Safe water mark   Mo 'A' (▪ ━)

Lighted offshore platform   Mo 'U' (▪ ▪ ━)

Fog signal – siren   Mo 'N' (━ ▪)

International Code of Signals

Some of the more common signals you may see are:

 I have a diver down. Keep clear

 I am taking on, discharging or carrying dangerous goods

 I require a pilot

 I have a pilot on board

 Man overboard

 My vessel is healthy and I require free pratique ('Quarantine' flag)

 You are running into danger

 I require assistance

 I am in distress and require immediate assistance

  Submarines are operating in this area. Proceed with caution

 Proceed at slow speed when passing

Weather patterns – a summary

Assessing the weather, present and forecast, is an essential skill for skippers of small craft, so this section is necessarily detailed. A working knowledge of the causes of weather patterns will help you to make your own evaluations and more accurately interpret professionally produced forecasts and charts.

Causes of weather patterns

Variations in weather conditions are the direct result of changes in temperature within the moist, dense air mass that envelops the Earth. The air exerts a pressure on the surface of the Earth, and atmospheric pressure at sea level, measured by barometer, averages 1013.2mb. Radiant energy from the sun heats the surface unevenly so that the atmosphere is warmer in some places than in others. Since warm air is less dense than cold air, it rises – cold air sinks to replace it – and variations above and below average pressure occur, resulting in regions of relatively high and low pressure.

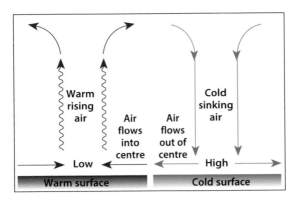

Weather patterns – a summary

Air always moves from a region of high pressure to one of lower pressure – but not directly because the movement is deflected by the rotation of the Earth. The flow of air is felt as wind whenever there is a difference in atmospheric pressure between two localities; its strength is determined by the rate of change in pressure between the two centres.

Wind belts

This convection process results in a pattern of pressure and wind belts around the Earth but there are local variations.

Generally, when air is moving down in an area of high pressure, the weather is dry and settled but, where the air is rising and pressure is low, the weather is disturbed because rising air cools, expands and condenses into cloud and this rising air draws in more of the surrounding air masses to fuel the process.

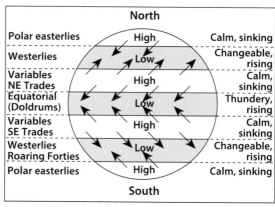

General circulation of the rotating Earth's atmosphere.

Barometric pressure

Variation in barometric pressure is one of the sailor's principal indications of impending changes to wind and weather.

In general, barometer steady or rising steadily indicates fair weather. Falling slowly indicates rain and possibly wind. Falling or rising rapidly indicates strong wind and probably rain.

Highs and lows

Anticyclones and *depressions* (highs and lows) are the two main weather systems of the middle latitudes. In the northern hemisphere, an anticyclone is a system where winds blow in a clockwise direction around areas of high pressure. The strongest winds blow round the outer extremities of the area and gradually diminish in strength towards the centre where they are light or non-existent.

Anticyclones are fair weather systems with moderate winds and reasonably clear skies. They are generally slow moving, sometimes remaining stationary for several days.

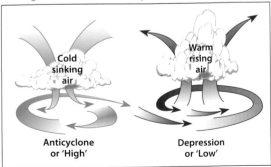

Anticyclone or 'High'

Depression or 'Low'

Depressions and their associated fronts are largely responsible for unsettled weather, strong winds and heavy rainfall. A depression is an area of low pressure around which the winds blow in an anti-clockwise direction in the northern hemisphere. They vary greatly in size and intensity and can move rapidly in any direction but most usually eastward.

Weather fronts

A 'front' is the boundary between two kinds of air. The main air masses that affect British waters originate from either the Polar or sub-tropical highs. Although classified according to its source, each air mass may arrive by different routes, therefore its properties will depend upon its path and the general kind of weather to be expected from each mass is:

- ◆ *Arctic and Polar* – cold
- ◆ *Tropical* – warm
- ◆ *Maritime* – wet
- ◆ *Continental* – dry

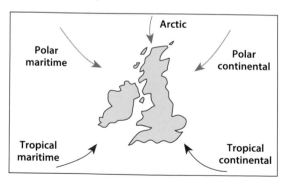

Most depressions that approach Britain form along the Polar front – the name given to the boundary between these two air masses.

Cold Polar air

Warm tropical air

Front with opposing air currents.

How depressions develop

When warm and cold air masses meet they interact and a wave develops in the front with its tip on the pole-ward side. Atmospheric pressure at the tip of the wave starts to fall until a complete circulation of air around a low pressure centre is established and a sector of warm air has become trapped in a squeeze between the cold air behind and the cool air ahead producing the fronts that are characteristic of a depression.

Depressions are bad weather systems with their most turbulent winds occurring at their centres, so it is an advantage to know where the centre of an approaching depression lies in relation to your own position.

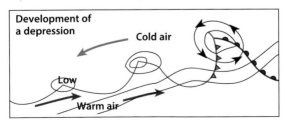

Development of a depression

Cold air

Low

Warm air

Weather maps

A weather map shows the distribution of atmospheric pressure throughout an area by means of lines (isobars) drawn through places having the same pressure. The isobaric structure in any area gives an indication of the weather pattern prevailing there. Isobars are drawn at intervals of 2, 4 or 8mb either side of 1000mb, thus forming a pressure contour map similar to a geographical contour map.

The pressure gradient is the rate of change in pressure across the isobars and is analogous to the gradient of a hill. Closely spaced land contours indicate steep gradients; similarly, closely spaced isobars portray steep pressure

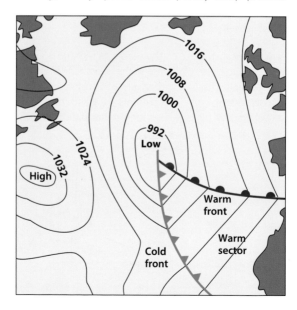

gradients which, in turn, produce stronger winds.

Each isobar forms a closed circuit around a centre of either high or low pressure. In the northern hemisphere, winds above 2000ft blow parallel to the isobars – clockwise around areas of high pressure and anti-clockwise around low pressure areas. Surface winds however are always 'backed' from the direction of the isobars and diverge away from a centre of high pressure but converge towards a centre of low pressure.

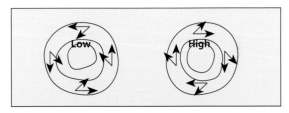

A simple depression in the northern hemisphere with winds blowing anti-clockwise in the general direction of the isobars but backed slightly inwards is shown below. From the centre, line A–B represents the warm front – the leading edge of the air in the warm sector, which is riding

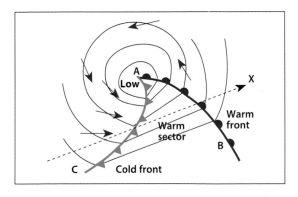

up over the relatively cold air to the right of it. Line A–C is the cold front. This is the leading edge of a wedge of cold air, which is pushing into the warm sector ahead of it. In this instance the depression and its fronts are moving steadily from left to right in the general direction of the isobars in the warm sector and if you were at 'X', you might expect to experience the following pattern of events as the depression passes over you.

High cloud from the west increases and lowers as the warm front approaches, pressure falls and the wind strengthens and backs; visibility deteriorates and light rain becomes continuous and heavy. As the warm front passes, pressure steadies, the wind veers, and rain stops or turns to drizzle. In the warm sector, visibility is poor, with drizzle or showers. Wind and pressure is steady. At the cold front, pressure falls then rises sharply. Wind veers and becomes squally with heavy rain. As the front moves away, rain stops, visibility improves and pressure rises.

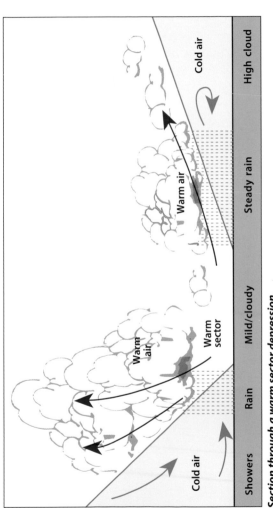

Section through a warm sector depression.

High cloud

Cold air

Warm air

Steady rain

Warm air

Mild/cloudy

Warm sector

Rain

Warm air

Showers

Cold air

Local effects

Wind is moving air created by temperature differences. Local winds in various forms are a modification to the general weather pattern but stem from the same basic cause.

Sea breezes These develop in coastal areas when convection over the land on a warm sunny day causes strong upward currents of air. The rising air is replaced by an inflow of air from over the sea which creates an onshore wind.

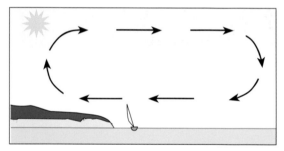

Land breeze At night the process is reversed. The Earth cools quickly after sunset while the sea retains its temperature and so air is drawn off the land to replace the warm air rising from over the sea.

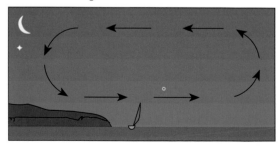

Katabatic winds

In areas where the coastline is more dramatic and cloudless skies at night result in radiation cooling of the land, a strong, down-slope wind can develop as air in contact with the ground becomes chilled and flows rapidly down the hillside.

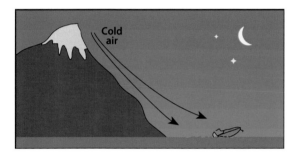

Fog This can form at any time of year but does so most frequently in late spring to mid-summer. It occurs when warm moist air is cooled sufficiently to become saturated and condense into water vapour.

Advection (sea fog) This occurs when warm moist air flows over a relatively cold sea surface and the temperature of the air in contact with this surface is lowered. If the sea temperature is below the dew point temperature of the air and cooling continues until the air is saturated, condensation will take place and form mist or fog.

Radiation (land fog) A clear night sky results in rapid cooling of the land. Should the surface temperature fall below the dew point temperature of the air, saturation will occur and condensation will take place with the formation of fog, which may drift out to sea.

Beaufort scale

Originally devised for larger sailing craft, this scale is only a rough guide to what may be expected in open water. Wind speeds are averages and gusts up to the next force should be anticipated. Sea conditions are generally more severe nearer to land and wave height can increase dramatically within minutes.

You should never venture outside sheltered waters unless you have obtained a current weather forecast and can interpret it correctly.

▶▶ *Caution*

The table opposite is a guide to what may be expected the open sea. Gusts may be at least one force higher than shown. Force 6 is often referred to as a yachtsman's gale – with good reason.

Beaufort wind force scale

Force	Knots	Wind	Probable sea state
0	0		Calm, glassy
1	1–3	Light airs	Calm, ripples
2	4–6	Light breeze	Small wavelets, not breaking
3	7–10	Gentle breeze	Larger wavelets, a few breaking
4	11–16	Mod breeze	Small waves, frequent white horses
5	17–21	Fresh breeze	Moderate waves, many white horses, some spray
6	22–27	Strong breeze	Large waves, white horses everywhere, spray
7	28–33	Near gale	Sea heaps up, waves breaking white foam blown in streaks
8	34–40	Gale	Moderately high waves, spindrift, white foam
9	41–47	Severe gale	High waves, tumbling crests, visibility affected by spray
10	48–55	Storm	Very high breaking waves, sea surface white, reduced visibility
11	56-63	Violent storm	Exceptionally high waves, visibility badly affected
12	64+	Hurricane	Air filled with foam, driving spray, very poor visibility

Shipping forecasts

General weather forecasts may be obtained from many sources, including TV, radio, internet and newspapers. Official Met Office shipping forecasts and inshore forecasts are promulgated as follows:

- **NAVTEX** is the primary method of disseminating Maritime Safety Information (MSI) broadcasts. The user can select which sea areas are selected for display and recording. Eliminates the risk of missing a forecast. A dedicated aerial and receiver are required.
- **MSI broadcasts** are transmitted every three hours by the coastguard on VHF. The content varies, but the inshore forecast is broadcast every three hours, and the full shipping forecast every 12 hours. Gale warnings are broadcast at the next scheduled MSI after receipt.

Details of times and frequencies are in *Reeds Nautical Almanac* and other almanacs. VHF Channels 10, 62, 63 and 64 are used, depending on your area. An initial announcement is made on Ch 16.

Online The Met Office website shows the land forecast as well as the shipping and inshore waters forecasts.

Harbour/marina offices usually display forecasts for the local area.

BBC In addition to the sources listed above, the shipping forecast is also broadcast on Radio 4 at 0048, 0520, 1201 and 1745. You need to remember to tune in and have pen and paper to hand. Frequencies are shown in *Reeds Nautical Almanac* and other almanacs.

WEATHER

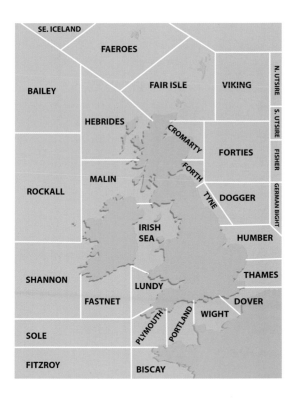

SE. ICELAND

FAEROES

BAILEY

FAIR ISLE

VIKING

N. UTSIRE

S. UTSIRE

FISHER

HEBRIDES

CROMARTY

FORTIES

GERMAN BIGHT

ROCKALL

MALIN

FORTH

TYNE

DOGGER

IRISH SEA

HUMBER

SHANNON

LUNDY

THAMES

FASTNET

DOVER

PLYMOUTH

PORTLAND

WIGHT

SOLE

FITZROY

BISCAY

Definitions

> ▶▶ **Note**
> The direction of the wind is given *from* where it is blowing. A southerly wind, therefore, is blowing from south to north.

Veer　　　　The wind is said to veer when it shifts to blow from a more clockwise direction. For example, it may veer from SW to NW.

Back　　　　The wind backs when it is shifts to blow from a more anti-clockwise direction. For example, it may back from SW to SE.

Imminent　　Gale force winds are expected within 6 hours.

Soon　　　　Gale force winds are expected in 6 to 12 hours.

Later　　　　Gale force winds are expected in 12 to 24 hours.

Good　　　　Visibility more than 5 miles.

Moderate　　Visibility 2 to 5 miles.

Poor　　　　Visibility between 1000 metres and 2 miles.

Fog　　　　Visibility less than 1000 metres.

Steady　　　Pressure has changed less than 0.1mb in last 3 hours.

Rising/falling slowly　　Pressure has changed 0.1mb to 1.5mb in last 3 hours.

Rising/falling	Pressure has changed 1.6mb to 3.5mb in last 3 hours.
Rising/falling quickly	Pressure has changed 3.6mb to 6.0mb in last 3 hours.
Rising/falling very rapidly	Pressure has changed more than 6.0mb in last 3 hours.
Now rising/ falling	Pressure was falling but is now rising (or vice versa).
Slowly	Weather system is moving at up to 15 knots.
Steadily	Weather system is moving at 15 to 25 knots.
Rather quickly	Weather system is moving at 25 to 35 knots.
Rapidly	Weather system is moving at 35 to 45 knots.
Very rapidly	Weather system is moving at over 45 knots.

Gale and strong wind warnings

Gale warnings are issued when the wind is expected to reach at least force 8 (with gusts up to 43 knots). They are broadcast at convenient programme breaks on BBC Radio 4 and by the coastguard on receipt.

Strong wind forecasts are included in all MSI broadcasts. They indicate that the wind will reach force 6 or above.

Choice of anchor

New designs of anchors are constantly being developed. Some of the common types are shown here. The names used are generic and don't necessarily indicate a particular manufacturer. Which one you choose will depend on your size of boat, usual cruising area and budget. No anchor is totally effective on all sea bedss, so your choice will inevitably be a compromise.

Generally, anchors hold best in firm mud, clay and sand but less well in soft mud, shingle and gravel. Holding is unreliable on a sea bed of rock or weed.

Most yachts carry a large main (bower) anchor and a smaller kedge anchor. This combination provides flexibility: the main anchor, for instance, in windy conditions and for overnight stays, while the kedge might be used for short stops in benign conditions. A kedge laid out astern can be used to prevent the boat swinging in a narrow river, for example.

Take advice on size/weight of anchor and chain for your boat.

Anchor types

Delta A good all-round anchor which holds very well on most sea beds. Several variations by different manufacturers.

Rocna/spade Excellent holding power. Expensive.

CQR Good in soft sand and mud but less reliable in hard sand or weed. Used to be popular but now largely superseded by more modern designs. Can be difficult to stow.

Bruce/Claw Good in most conditions but might struggle in clay and hard mud. Can be difficult to stow.

Danforth/fluke Good in soft sand and mud but not in most other sea beds. May be a good choice for smaller boats. Stows flat.

Anchoring

Choose your anchorage Look at the type of sea bed and depth of water, and allow plenty of swinging room. Anchor well clear of other boats.

Recommended anchorages are shown on some charts by a small anchor symbol. This indicates a general area, *not* an exact position.

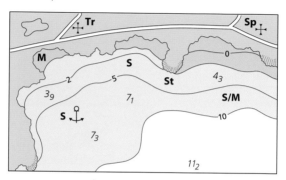

Depth of water Work out the maximum height of tide during your stay and add it to the charted depth to determine the amount of cable to use.

Work out the minimum depth of water during your stay to ensure a sufficient safety margin under the keel.

Letting go Try to anchor into the wind or tidal stream – whichever has the most influence on your boat. Look how other similar boats are lying.

Let go the anchor when the boat is stopped or gathering slight sternway. In a tidal stream or brisk wind, allow the boat to fall back to dig in the anchor. In calm conditions you might need to use the engine in astern.

Cable As a rule of thumb, use 3–4 times the maximum depth of water for a chain cable, and 6 times the depth for rope. If staying overnight in windy conditions, use more; for a short lunchtime stay in calm conditions, 2–3 times the depth may be sufficient.

Anchor bearings When the boat has settled down, fix your position so you can check if the anchor starts to drag. Natural transits ashore are particularly useful.

If you swing with the tide, re-check the bearings/transits when lying on the new heading.

Shapes/lights Hoist the anchor ball in the fore part of the boat when it can best be seen. At night, show an all-round white anchor light. In a yacht anchorage, a lantern at eye level (about 3 metres above the waterline) is more easily seen than a masthead light.

Using two anchors

A boat lying to a single anchor will have a large swinging circle. In crowded anchorages in calm conditions, the circle can be reduced by using two anchors laid out over the bow with the heaviest anchor towards the strongest tidal stream.

Drop the main anchor as before and allow the boat to drift back as you pay out **twice** the required length of cable. Lower the second anchor and pull the boat forward again by hauling in the main cable while paying out the second anchor's cable until the boat is positioned midway between the two anchors. Make the second cable fast to the main cable and let them out until the joint is **well below the depth of the keel**.

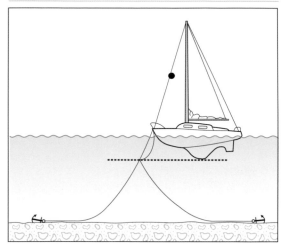

▶▶ Caution
In strong cross winds both anchors may drag.

Windy conditions
When strong winds are expected, and the boat will be wind-rode rather than tide-rode, a safer method of lying to two anchors is to drop the main anchor as before, allow the boat to drift back to set the anchor, and then

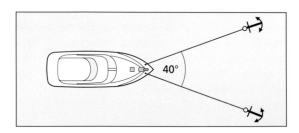

✱ Tip

To secure a cable (rope or chain) to a samson post, take three turns round the post, pass a bight of cable under the part attached to the anchor and slip it over the turns on the post. For extra security, take the end round the post again and repeat the process with a second bight of cable. A rope or chain secured in this way will not jam and can be released under load.

motor off at an angle of about 40° to the line of the first anchor and drop the kedge level with it. Allow the boat to drift back again, then adjust and cleat the cables securely.

Fouled anchor

Never anchor near underwater cables or pipelines and avoid places on the chart marked 'Foul Ground' where there will be obstructions upon which an anchor might become fast.

An anchor buoy with a trip line attached to the crown of the anchor will provide a means of freeing it, but it is not unknown for an unwary skipper to try to moor to someone else's anchor buoy. There is also a danger that the line may foul your rudder at low water and trip the anchor later as the tide rises. For these reasons, you may prefer to lash the tripping line to your anchor cable and bring the buoy back on board.

Anchoring

If you have no tripping line set and the anchor becomes fast, haul the cable in until it is vertical and taut, take a turn around a cleat, move all the crew right aft and see if the motion of the boat will break it out. If not, try motoring in the opposite direction from which the anchor was originally set or veer a little more cable then, keeping it taut, motor in a circle around your anchor to see if that will free it.

Berthing alongside

Fenders Whether your berth is alongside a pontoon, wall or another boat, rig plenty of (clean) fenders. Have them high up if berthing an another boat.

There is no need to rig fenders on your outboard side as they may snag the fenders of a boat berthing on you. You can always slip in some extra ones later if necessary.

Ropes You need at least four mooring lines. Avoid ones with a spliced eye in one end – it will invariably be at the wrong end – and have them all the same length so any line may be used for any job. The four lines are:

• Bow rope (aka headrope).
• Stern rope. Consider rigging it from the *outboard* quarter for a better lead.
• Fore spring – which prevents the boat moving ahead.
• Back spring – which prevents the boat moving astern.

In some conditions, breast ropes may also be rigged but, as they will be relatively short, they are liable to snatch.

Use only one rope for one job. This will make leaving the berth much easier, and is usually more secure.

If necessary, particularly for a long stay, protect your ropes by wrapping them with cloth or pass them through a short length of plastic tubing where they rub on fairleads or other surfaces.

In rough or windy conditions, the use of rubber snubbers will help to reduce snatching.

Cleats The simplest way of securing a rope to a cleat is to drop a bowline over it, and take any surplus line back onto the boat.

- *Never* use 'figures of eight' on a cleat which may be used by someone else.
- Don't pass a rope through a cleat – it is liable to jam when letting go.
- Before leaving, re-rig the lines round the cleat a back onboard so that they may be slipped from inboard.

Rings and bollards

A line is best attached to a mooring ring with a round turn and two half hitches. This knot is very secure and can be released while under tension.

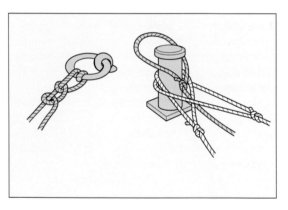

A bowline is best for making fast to a bollard or cleat, but always pass the loop up through any others that are there already. The lines can then be released in any order just by lifting the appropriate loop off the bollard or cleat and dropping it back through the others.

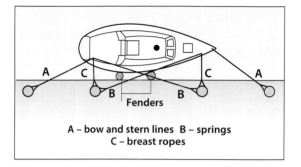

A – bow and stern lines B – springs
C – breast ropes

Shore lines Use the same ropes as for berthing on a pontoon, but also rig long lines ashore. These should take the strain of your boat and prevent undue load on the inboard boat's lines and cleats. When rigged, ease off the bow and stern lines to the inboard boat.

Slipping When departing, remove the shore lines and rig the other lines as slips so that they can be let go from your own boat.

ANCHORING AND BERTHING

Berthing alongside another boat

It doesn't usually matter which way you face in relation to the other boat. Ask permission to come alongside and head into the strongest element: wind or tide. Provide adequate fenders; rig springs and breast ropes to the other boat and haul them tight. If the boats are facing the same way, adjust the springs to put the masts out of line in case the boats roll. Take your own bow and stern lines ashore, and be sure they take their fair share of the strain. Ease out the breast ropes to the inboard boat if necessary.

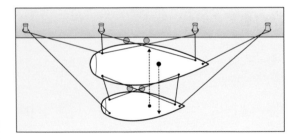

If the face of the wall is rough or made of piles, you will need to rig a fender board to bridge the gaps and to protect your fenders.

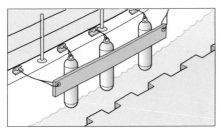

✳ Tip

If you expect to be away from the boat while the tide is ebbing and you are uncertain about the range of tide at your mooring, or the amount of slack you need to leave in the lines, just make a bight in one of the lines and double it, then put on a 'seizing' of some easily breaking stuff such as ordinary string. If the lines are then subject to any undue strain, the string will break and allow another metre or so of slack.

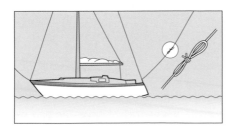

Leaving a berth

Leaving an alongside berth when there is little or no wind or tidal stream

If your boat is berthed closely between other boats and you are short-handed, or your boat is too heavy to push off with the boathook, try 'springing off' using your engine and a suitable mooring line.

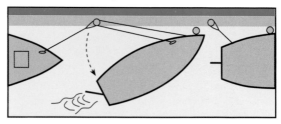

Rig your bow spring as a 'slip' and position a fender well forward between the bow and the quay. Gently engage ahead with rudder turned towards the quay and the stern will begin to swing out. Once you are clear of the boat behind, slip and retrieve the spring and reverse away.

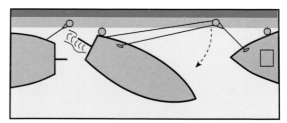

Rig a stern spring as a 'slip' and position a fender well aft between the boat and the quay. Centralise the rudder and gently engage astern drive. The bow will begin to swing out and when it is clear of the boat ahead, slip and retrieve the spring and motor ahead and away.

Using the tidal stream to leave an alongside berth

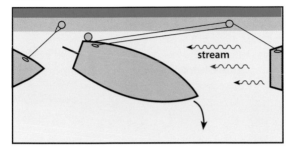

With the tidal stream on the bow, position a fender aft and rig the stern spring as a 'slip'. Remove the bow lines and the effect of the tidal stream will cause the bow to swing out. When clear of any boat ahead, engage ahead, slip and retrieve the stern spring and motor ahead and away.

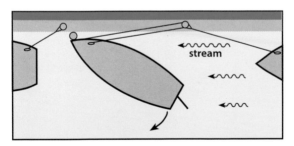

With the tidal stream from astern, position a fender well forward and rig the bow spring as a 'slip'. Remove the stern lines and the effect of the tidal stream will cause the stern to swing out. When clear of any boat behind you, engage astern propulsion, slip and retrieve the bow spring and reverse away.

Leaving a raft of boats

To leave from a berth in the middle of a raft of boats, you must rearrange the mooring lines of the adjacent boats so that you can leave in the direction of the strongest element (wind or tide) so that its force will cause the other boats to swing together as you leave. If you attempt to leave **against a strong wind or tide**, the raft will be torn apart and boats may be damaged.

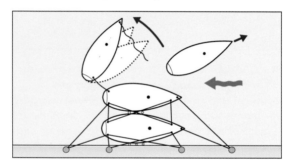

To leave a raft (bows first)

1 Have your engine running in neutral. Take in your bow and stern lines, remove your springs from the inside boat and make up the breast ropes as slip lines.
2 Unfasten the bow line of the boat lying outside you and lead it right round your own boat, outside the guardrail and shrouds and back to the shore, extending the line if necessary.
3 Cast off the springs and breast ropes of the outside boat, make a final check for any forgotten ropes, snagged fenders, or rope dangling in the water, then slip your breast ropes from the inside boat and gently ease your boat out with the current. If there is no one aboard the other boats to help you, you will have to leave one of your crew behind to secure their lines, and pick him/her up later.

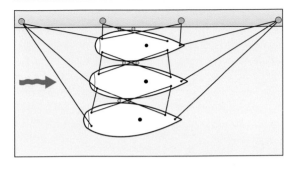

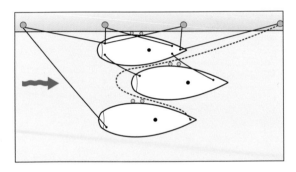

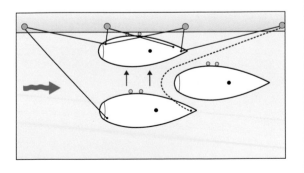

Theory of sailing

It is possible to sail upwind because the boat's sails assume an aerofoil shape when the wind fills them. Air flowing over the curved leeward side of the sail accelerates, decreasing the pressure on that surface and creating a partial vacuum or suction effect called 'lift', which tends to drive the boat forward.

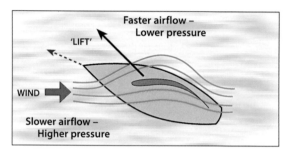

Wind pressure on the other side of the sail gives it its curved shape and also creates a force that tries to push the boat downwind. But this sideways movement (leeway) is resisted by the keel and rudder and so the forward 'lift' of the sail predominates and, combined with a similar forward 'lift' generated by the keel, which functions as a 'hydrofoil', the boat is driven in that direction.

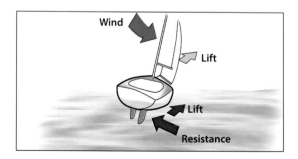

The faster that the air can be made to flow over the curved surface of a sail, the greater will be the 'lift' created. This condition is met, when beating or reaching, by an overlap between the headsail and the luff of the main, which creates a 'slot effect' to squeeze and speed up the airflow through the gap between the sails.

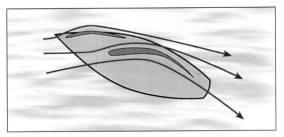

In general, the narrower the slot, the faster the airflow, but this must not be overdone or the airstream from the leech of the headsail will 'backwind' the luff of the mainsail and destroy its lift completely.

The mainsail needs to be sheeted in slightly harder than the headsail, but try to keep the slot between the two sails even so that their leeches follow a similar curve.

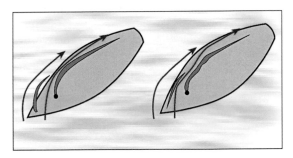

Apparent wind

All moving vehicles experience a 'speed wind' blowing in the opposite direction to that in which the vehicle is moving.

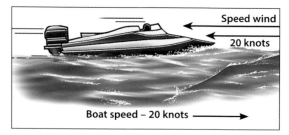

Even on a windless day, a cyclist will feel a wind on his face caused solely by his movement through the still air and the faster he pedals, the stronger that wind will become.

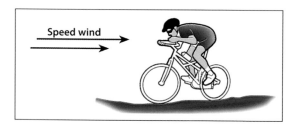

On a windy day, the wind that is felt by the crew of a moving yacht is a combination of the true wind and the speed wind and is known as the 'apparent wind'. This is the wind to which the sails are trimmed and its direction is invariably forward of the true wind's direction.

When sailing, the apparent wind is important as it determines how the sails are trimmed to best advantage.

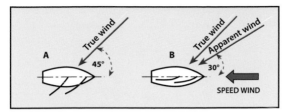

Most boats are unable to sail closer than about 45° to the true wind **A** but once the boat begins to move and pick up speed, the apparent wind strengthens and moves forward and the sails are trimmed accordingly as in **B**.

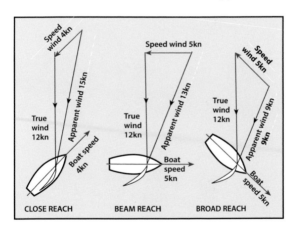

Given a true wind of constant velocity, the velocity and direction of the apparent wind varies with the speed of the vessel and its point of sailing, as shown by the vector diagrams.

Points of sailing

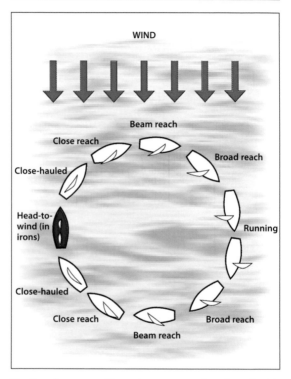

Starting from a position where you are heading directly into the wind, the following terms are used:

In irons   Head-to-wind; sailing flapping uselessly; no steerage way.

Close-hauled Sailing as close to the wind as possible with the sails full.

Close reach   Further off the wind than close-hauled but not as far as a beam reach.

Beam reach   Sailing with the wind at roughly at 90° to the boat's heading.

Broad reach   Between a beam reach and running.

Running   Sailing directly down wind.

On any of these points of sailing (except when in irons), the wind will either be blowing over the port side (*port tack*) or the starboard side (*starboard tack*). When running, the tack you are on is the opposite to the side the mainsail (or largest sail if the mainsail is not set) is set.

Definitions

Bends   Used to join two rope ends.

Hitches   Used to secure ropes to objects.

Knots   Not a bend or a hitch!

Bowline Probably the most common and useful knot for sailors. It forms a bight (loop) in the end of as rope and, once mastered, is quick to tie, will not jam and can easily be undone if not under load.

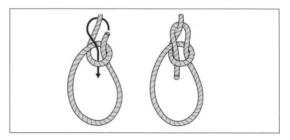

Clove hitch Most commonly used to secure fenders to guardrails, but is not ideal as it can slip when subject to loads, particularly when the ends are pulled sideways. Also used for securing any line to a spar or post.

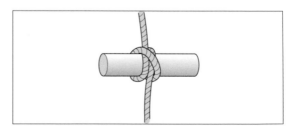

Fisherman's bend Good for securing a line to a ring or an anchor. It will not jam, and can easily be released even when it has been under load.

Figure of eight knot Tied at the end of any line to prevent it passing through a sheeve. Should always be used on sheets.

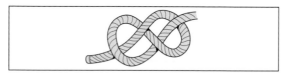

Reef knot Although a common knot, it can be surprisingly insecure, mainly if used to join two lines of different sizes and/or materials. Can be difficult to undo.

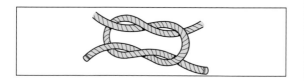

Definitions

Rolling hitch Good for securing a line to a spar or another rope when the direction of pull is along the spar or rope. Similar to a clove hitch but with an additional turn.

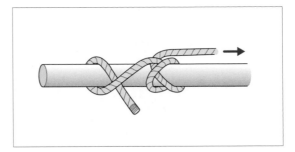

Round turn and two half hitches Much more secure for fenders on guardrails. Also used for securing a rope to a post or bollard. Be sure to make a full turn round the object not just a half hitch which is not at all secure.

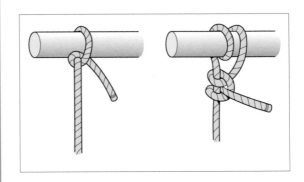

Sheepshank Shortens a rope temporarily. Can fall apart if not under load.

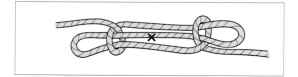

Sheet bend Good for securing a small rope to a larger rope. Can fall apart if not under load. A double sheet bend is more secure.

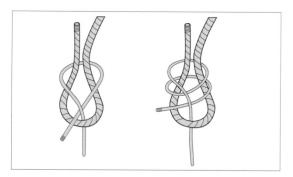

Securing to a cleat

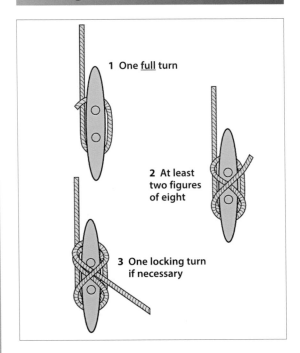

1 One <u>full</u> turn

2 At least two figures of eight

3 One locking turn if necessary

- Start with one full turn round the cleat.
- Make at least two figures of eight. Three are usually sufficient, any more just take up more room on the cleat. Do not use locking turns on each figure of eight – they can jam.
- Finish with just one locking turn to tidy up the end if necessary.

Rope materials

There are many types of rope, all with different characteristics and for different uses. To get the best life from your ropes, wash them frequently in fresh water to get rid of salt and grit.

Some of the most common ropes found at sea are:

Manila A natural fibre not often seen in modern yachts but used widely in traditional boats. It is strong and flexible, but absorbs water and shrinks when wet.

Polypropylene Synthetic material which is widely used afloat. It is hard wearing and floats, but does not have good resistance to UV light.

Nylon Synthetic material which is strong and relatively elastic. Good for anchoring, mooring and towing. Does not float.

Polyester Almost a strong as nylon but not as elastic. Often used for halyards, sheets and reefing lines.

HMPE (aka **Dyneema**) Very strong with good resistance to abrasion and UV light. Many uses afloat but expensive.

UK waterways

Inland waterways include any area of water not categorised as 'sea', eg canals, tidal and non-tidal rivers, lakes, and some estuarial waters (an arm of sea that extends inland to meet the mouth of a river).

While the UK's inland waterways are generally, but not exclusively, used by leisure craft, the inland waterways of mainland Europe are used extensively by large commercial vessels. There are different rules for each.

If you want to take a boat onto inland waterways in the UK, you will need to register her, obtain a licence and have her inspected for a **Boat Safety Scheme (BSS) Certificate**. The BSS is a public safety initiative owned equally by the Canal & River Trust and the Environment Agency.

All other aspects of using a boat on the waterways are comprehensively covered in the Canal & River Trust's **Boater's Handbook.** There you will find clear advice including:

- Boat handling.
- Boating safety.
- Rules for the waterways.
- Good boating behaviour.

European waterways

The code which governs navigation on all the interconnected waterways of Europe is Le Code Européen des Voies de Navigation Intérieure (CEVNI).

Before visiting European inland waterways by boat you must have a CEVNI qualification which is issued by the RYA following a short test. You must also carry onboard a copy of the CEVNI handbook.

Below are just some of the signs and signals you may encounter. Full details can be found in *The RYA European Waterways Regulations* and *The RYA CEVNI Handbook*.

Signals indicating side to pass

NIGHT

 or

Pass slowly on either side. DO NOT CREATE WASH.

NIGHT

 or

Pass only on the side displaying red and white flags or a red and white board. DO NOT CREATE WASH.

NIGHT

 or

Pass only on the side displaying green bi-cones or a green and white board.

NIGHT

 or

It is safe to pass on either side.

▶▶ Caution

Do not confuse the passage-prohibited sign ▬ with the sign ▬ which permits passage without creating wash.

CEVNI – red waterway signs

General prohibitory signs

ENTRY OR PASSAGE
FORBIDDEN

NO ACCESS EXCEPT FOR
NON-MOTORISED SMALL CRAFT

Specific prohibitions – *Red diagonal bar*

NO OVERTAKING

NO PASSING OR
OVERTAKING

NO TURNING

NO ANCHORING

NO MOORING

NO BERTHING

NO MOTORISED
VESSELS

NO ROWING BOATS
OR CANOES

NO SAILING

Mandatory – *Prescribed course*

GO IN DIRECTION
OF ARROW

MOVE TO LEFT
OF CHANNEL

MOVE TO RIGHT
OF CHANNEL

KEEP TO LEFT
OF CHANNEL

KEEP TO RIGHT
OF CHANNEL

CROSS CHANNEL
TO PORT

CROSS CHANNEL
TO STBD

▶▶ Important

These abridged notes and illustrations should only be used in conjunction with those given in the official CEVNI handbook.

Restrictions and mandatory instructions

DEPTH LIMIT
(190cm)

HEADROOM LIMITED
(6m)

PASSAGE CHANNEL
WIDTH (18m)

CHANNEL 12m
FROM BANK

SPEED LIMIT
(6kph

KEEP A SHARP
LOOK-OUT

STOP AS
NECESSARY

SOUND HORN

GIVE WAY TO VESSELS USING MAJOR WATERWAY AHEAD

NAVIGATION RESTRICTED
MAKE ENQUIRIES

Additional information panels

SPEED LIMIT
8kph IN 500m

BEWARE –
FERRY AHEAD

STOP – CUSTOMS

NO BERTHING
WITHIN 10m

NO ANCHORING FOR
NEXT 500m

STRONG CROSS
CURRENT – 150m

CEVNI – blue informative and advisory signs

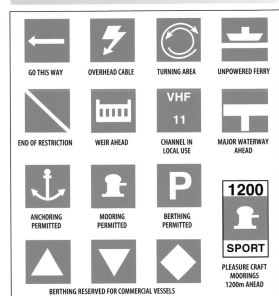

GO THIS WAY	OVERHEAD CABLE	TURNING AREA	UNPOWERED FERRY
END OF RESTRICTION	WEIR AHEAD	CHANNEL IN LOCAL USE	MAJOR WATERWAY AHEAD
ANCHORING PERMITTED	MOORING PERMITTED	BERTHING PERMITTED	PLEASURE CRAFT MOORINGS 1200m AHEAD

BERTHING RESERVED FOR COMMERCIAL VESSELS

Special berthing signs

Vessels displaying blue cones by day or blue lights at night have dangerous cargoes and special berths distinguished by blue triangles are reserved for these vessels.

Do not berth within 10m of a sign with one blue triangle, within 50m of a sign with two triangles, or within 100m of a sign with three triangles.

CEVNI – light signals at locks and opening bridges

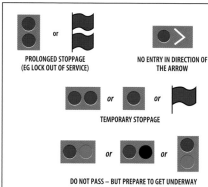

PROLONGED STOPPAGE
(EG LOCK OUT OF SERVICE)

NO ENTRY IN DIRECTION OF
THE ARROW

TEMPORARY STOPPAGE

DO NOT PASS – BUT PREPARE TO GET UNDERWAY

Red and green lights control passage under moveable bridges. When yellow lights are shown in conjunction with red lights, passage is permitted for vessels of reduced height.

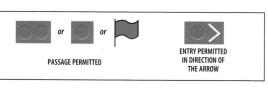

PASSAGE PERMITTED

ENTRY PERMITTED
IN DIRECTION OF
THE ARROW

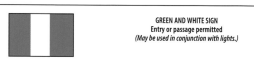

GREEN AND WHITE SIGN
Entry or passage permitted
(May be used in conjunction with lights.)

CEVNI – land marks and cross-overs

Land marks

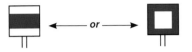

Red and white top marks on posts indicate that the channel lies close to the right bank – the bank on your right-hand side as you travel down stream ('down hill' on a canal).

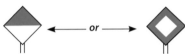

Green and white top marks on posts indicate that the channel lies close to the left bank – the bank on your left-hand side as you travel down stream ('down hill' on a canal).

Lights – if fitted – are rhythmic red or green as appropriate.

RIGHT BANK MARKS

LEFT BANK MARKS

Cross-overs

A post with either a yellow or a yellow and black top mark indicates the place where the channel crosses from one bank to the other.

Lights – when fitted – are yellow. Group flashing (2) or occulting with even number characteristics on the right bank.

Group flashing (3) or occulting with odd number characteristics on the left bank.

CEVNI – fixed bridge markings

Bridges with channels too narrow to allow the simultaneous passage of two or more vessels are marked with either red and white or green and white diamonds.

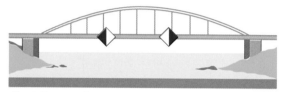

Fig 1 Passage is PROHIBITED in the area outside the white triangles.

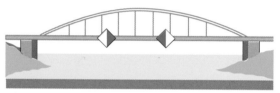

Fig 2 It is RECOMMENDED that vessels remain within the area between the green triangles.

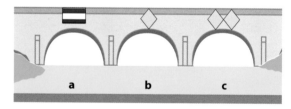

Fig 3a Red and white No entry/No passage sign. The span is closed to traffic travelling in this direction.
Fig 3b A single yellow diamond. The recommended route for all vessels. The span is open to traffic in both directions.
Fig 3c Two yellow diamonds. The span is open for vessels travelling in this direction, but is closed to vessels coming the other way.

Although GPS gives an accurate indication of your speed and distance *over the ground*, a properly calibrated log is still essential when, for instance, working up an EP or plotting a running fix when you need distance *through the water*. The speed and distance readouts of the log are directly related, so if the log is over-reading for one, it will be over-reading by the same percentage for the other.

There are two methods of calibrating (or checking) your log – measured distance and GPS – which are detailed below.

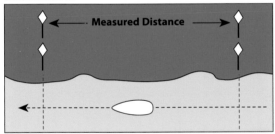

Methods

Measured distance

You will come across charted *measured distances* around the coast. They are pairs of transits which are usually, but not always, one mile apart. The actual distance will be shown on the chart. Alternatively, you can use any two fixed marks which are a known distance apart.

* Motor past the first mark or transit on the heading shown on the chart, and at a steady speed. Take the time (or start a stopwatch).
* As you pass the second mark, note the time again (or stop the watch).
* Calculate your speed over the ground: speed = distance ÷ time.
  Example: 1 mile in 12 minutes (ie 0.2 hour) gives a speed of 5 knots.

Compare this with the speed shown on the log and note the difference to determine by how much it is over- or under-reading. Consult the handbook to adjust the log.

If there is any tidal stream, repeat this in the opposite direction and take the average of the calculated speeds.

Global Positioning System

Simply comparing the GPS speed (SOG) against the log speed (speed through the water) will give a good indication of any error – but only if there is no tidal stream. The advantage of this method is that you can check it at any time without having to motor a pre-determined distance.

To check the accuracy of the log against a measured distance

For each run made, record: ● *Speed indicated by the log*
● *Distance recorded by the log*
● *Actual time taken*

Complete the boxes below and compare the total distance recorded by the log for runs 1 and 2 against the measured distance to obtain the log error. Compare the average speed found against the log's recorded speed to find the log error.

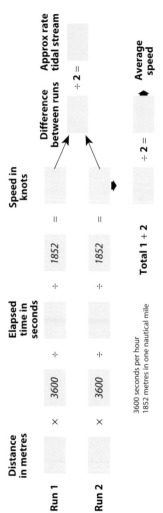

	Distance in metres		Elapsed time in seconds		Speed in knots		Difference between runs	Approx rate tidal stream
Run 1		× 3600		÷	1852	=		÷ 2 =
Run 2		× 3600		÷	1852	=		

3600 seconds per hour
1852 metres in one nautical mile

Total 1 + 2 ÷ 2 = ← Average speed

203

International code of signals

A – ALPHA
I have a diver down.
Keep clear
• ▬

*B – BRAVO
I am taking on,
discharging or carrying
dangerous goods
▬ • • •

*E – ECHO
I am altering course
to starboard
•

F – FOXTROT
I am disabled.
Communicate with me
• • ▬ •

*I – INDIA
I am altering my course
to port
• •

J – JULIETT
I am on fire and have
dangerous cargo aboard.
Keep clear
• ▬ ▬ ▬

*M – MIKE
My vessel is stopped
and making no way
through the water
▬ ▬

N – NOVEMBER
No
▬ •

Q – QUEBEC
My vessel is healthy and
I require free pratique
('Quarantine' flag)

R – ROMEO
• ▬ •

U – UNIFORM
You are running
into danger
• • ▬

V – VICTOR
I require assistance
• • • ▬

Y – YANKEE
I am dragging
my anchor
▬ • ▬ ▬

*Z – ZULU
I require a tug.
By fishing vessels
'I am shooting nets'
▬ ▬ • •

Second
Substitute

Third
Substitute

2 TOO
• • ▬ ▬ ▬

3 TREE
• • • ▬ ▬

6 SIX
▬ • • • •

7 SEV-EN
▬ ▬ • • •

*C – CHARLIE
Yes
— · — · ·

*D – DELTA
Keep clear of me. I am manoeuvring with difficulty
— · ·

*G – GOLF
I require a pilot. When made by fishing vessels 'I am hauling in nets'
— — ·

*H – HOTEL
I have a pilot on board
· · · ·

K – KILO
I wish to communicate with you
— · —

L – LIMA
You should stop your vessel instantly
· — · ·

O – OSCAR
Man overboard
— — —

P – PAPA
Vessel about to put to sea. By fishing vessels 'My nets are caught fast'
· — — ·

*S – SIERRA
My engines are going astern
· · ·

*T – TANGO
Keep clear of me; I am engaged in pair trawling
—

W – WHISKEY
I require medical assistance
· — —

X – X-RAY
Stop carrying out your intentions and watch for my signals
— · · —

Code and answering pennant

First Substitute

0 ZERO
— — — — —

1 WUN
· — — — —

4 FOW-ER
· · · · —

5 FIFE
· · · · ·

8 AIT
— — — · ·

9 NIN-ER
— — — — ·

International port traffic signals

No	Lights		Main message
1		Flashing	Serious emergency – All vessels to stop or divert according to instructions
2			Vessels shall not proceed (*Note*: Some ports may use an exemption signal, as in 2a below)
3		Fixed or Slow Occulting	Vessels may proceed. One-way traffic
4			Vessels may proceed. Two-way traffic
5			A vessel may proceed only when they have received specific orders to do so. (Note: Some ports may use an exemption signal, as in 5a below)

Exemption signals and messages

No	Lights		Main message
2a		Fixed or Slow Occulting	Vessels shall not proceed, except that vessels which navigate outside the main channel need not comply with the main message
5a			A vessel may proceed when they have received specific orders to do so, except that vessels which navigate outside the main channel need not comply with the main message

Auxiliary signals and messages

White and/or yellow lights, displayed to the right of the main lights	Local meanings, as promulgated in local port orders

Time, speed, distance

$$\frac{\text{Distance} \times 60}{\text{Speed}} = \textit{Time} \text{ (in minutes)}$$

$$\frac{\text{Distance} \times 60}{\text{Time}} = \textit{Speed} \text{ (in knots)}$$

$$\frac{\text{Speed} \times \text{Time}}{60} = \textit{Distance} \text{ (in nautical miles)}$$

The 10ths rule

In 6 minutes (1/10 hour) you will cover 1/10 of your speed in miles. So, at 6 knots you will cover 0.6 miles; at 12 knots you will cover 1.2 miles. In 3 minutes you will cover half that distance; in 12 minutes twice the distance. Remember to allow for any tidal stream.

Dutchman's Log

A rough estimate of boat speed can be obtained by noting the time it takes to travel its own length past a stationary object in the water.

$$\textit{Speed in knots} = \frac{\text{Length in metres}}{\text{Time in seconds}} \times 1.94$$

OR

$$\textit{Speed in knots} = \frac{\text{Length in feet}}{\text{Time in seconds}} \times 0.59$$

Distance off/Conversion/Sun movement

Distance off by vertical sextant angle

$$\text{Dist Off (n miles)} = \frac{1.852 \times \text{ht in metres}}{\text{angle in mins of arc}}$$

Distance of visible horizon (n miles):
$\sqrt{\text{Ht of eye (metres)}} \times 2.075$

One nautical mile	=	1.852 kilometres
	=	1.15078 statute miles
	=	6076.12 feet
	=	1852 metres
	=	10 cables

Conversion factors

Feet to metres	multiply by	0.3048
Metres to feet	"	3.2808
NM to statute miles	"	1.1515
Statute miles to NM	"	0.8684
Knots to mph	"	1.1515
Mph to knots	"	0.8684
Knots to km/h	"	1.8519
Km/h to knots	"	0.5400
Sq ft to sq m	"	0.0929
Sq m to sq ft	"	10.7643
Litres to pints	"	1.7600
Litres to gallons	"	0.2200
Pints to litres	"	0.5683
Gallons to litres	"	4.5460
1 Gallon (UK)	=	4.546 litres
1 Gallon (USA)	=	3.785 litres

Apparent movement of the sun

1° in 4 minutes
15° in 1 hour
360° in 24 hours

Distance off by vertical angle

Dist in miles	Height in metres									
	10	20	30	40	50	60	70	80	90	100
	Vertical angle									
0.1	3° 05'	6° 10'	9° 12'	12° 11'	15° 06'	17° 56'	20° 42'	23° 21'	25° 54'	28° 21'
0.2	1 33	3 05	4 38	6 10	7 41	9 12	10 42	12 11	13 39	15 06
0.3	1 02	2 04	3 05	4 07	5 08	6 10	7 11	8 11	9 12	10 12
0.4	0 46	1 33	2 19	3 05	3 52	4 38	5 24	6 10	6 55	7 41
0.5	0 37	1 14	1 51	2 28	3 05	3 42	4 19	4 56	5 33	6 10
0.6	0 31	1 02	1 33	2 04	2 34	3 05	3 36	4 07	4 38	5 08
0.7	0 27	0 53	1 19	1 46	2 12	2 39	3 05	3 32	3 58	4 24
0.8	0 23	0 46	1 10	1 33	1 56	2 19	2 42	3 05	3 28	3 52
0.9	0 21	0 41	1 02	1 22	1 43	2 04	2 24	2 45	3 05	3 26
1.0	0 19	0 37	0 56	1 14	1 33	1 51	2 10	2 28	2 47	3 05
1.1	0 17	0 34	0 51	1 07	1 24	1 41	1 58	2 15	2 32	2 49
1.2	0 15	0 31	0 46	1 02	1 17	1 33	1 48	2 04	2 19	2 34
1.3	0 14	0 29	0 43	0 57	1 11	1 26	1 40	1 54	2 08	2 23
1.4	0 13	0 27	0 40	0 53	1 06	1 19	1 33	1 46	1 59	2 12
1.5	0 12	0 25	0 37	0 49	1 02	1 14	1 27	1 39	1 51	2 04
1.6	0 12	0 23	0 35	0 46	0 58	1 10	1 21	1 33	1 44	1 56
1.7	0 11	0 22	0 33	0 44	0 55	1 05	1 16	1 27	1 38	1 49
1.8	0 10	0 21	0 31	0 41	0 52	1 02	1 12	1 22	1 33	1 43
1.9	0 10	0 20	0 29	0 39	0 49	0 59	1 08	1 18	1 28	1 38
2.0	0 09	0 19	0 28	0 37	0 46	0 56	1 05	1 14	1 23	1 33
2.1	0 09	0 18	0 27	0 35	0 44	0 53	0 53	1 11	1 19	1 28
2.2	0 08	0 17	0 25	0 34	0 42	0 51	0 59	1 07	1 16	1 24
2.3	0 08	0 16	0 24	0 32	0 40	0 48	0 56	1 05	1 13	1 21
2.4	0 08	0 15	0 23	0 31	0 39	0 46	0 54	1 02	1 10	1 17
2.5	0 07	0 15	0 22	0 30	0 37	0 45	0 52	0 59	1 07	1 14
2.6	0 07	0 14	0 21	0 29	0 36	0 43	0 50	0 57	1 04	1 11
2.7	0 07	0 14	0 21	0 27	0 34	0 41	0 48	0 55	1 02	1 09
2.8	0 07	0 13	0 20	0 27	0 33	0 40	0 46	0 53	1 00	1 06
2.9	0 06	0 13	0 19	0 26	0 32	0 38	0 45	0 51	0 58	1 04
3.0	0 06	0 12	0 19	0 25	0 31	0 37	0 43	0 49	0 56	1 02
3.1	0 06	0 12	0 18	0 24	0 30	0 36	0 42	0 48	0 54	1 00
3.2	0 06	0 12	0 17	0 23	0 29	0 35	0 41	0 46	0 52	0 58
3.3	0 06	0 11	0 17	0 22	0 28	0 34	0 39	0 45	0 51	0 56
3.4	0 05	0 11	0 16	0 22	0 27	0 33	0 38	0 44	0 49	0 55
3.5	0 05	0 11	0 16	0 21	0 27	0 32	0 37	0 42	0 48	0 53
3.6	0 05	0 10	0 15	0 21	0 26	0 31	0 35	0 41	0 46	0 52
3.7	0 05	0 10	0 15	0 20	0 25	0 30	0 35	0 40	0 45	0 50
3.8	0 05	0 10	0 15	0 20	0 24	0 29	0 34	0 39	0 44	0 49
3.9	0 05	0 10	0 14	0 19	0 24	0 29	0 33	0 38	0 43	0 48
4.0	0 05	0 09	0 14	0 19	0 23	0 28	0 32	0 37	0 42	0 46
4.1	0 05	0 09	0 14	0 18	0 23	0 27	0 32	0 35	0 41	0 45
4.2	0 04	0 09	0 13	0 18	0 22	0 27	0 31	0 35	0 40	0 44
4.3	0 04	0 09	0 13	0 17	0 22	0 26	0 30	0 35	0 39	0 43
4.4	0 04	0 08	0 13	0 17	0 21	0 25	0 30	0 34	0 38	0 42
4.5	0 04	0 08	0 12	0 16	0 21	0 24	0 29	0 33	0 37	0 41
4.6	0 04	0 08	0 12	0 16	0 20	0 24	0 28	0 32	0 36	0 40
4.7	0 04	0 08	0 12	0 16	0 20	0 24	0 28	0 32	0 36	0 39
4.8	0 04	0 08	0 12	0 15	0 19	0 23	0 27	0 31	0 35	0 39
4.9	0 04	0 08	0 11	0 15	0 19	0 23	0 27	0 30	0 34	0 38
5.0	0 04	0 07	0 11	0 15	0 19	0 22	0 25	0 30	0 33	0 37
	32.8	65.6	98.41	131.2	164.0	196.8	229.7	262.5	295.3	328.1

Range of lights

Distance of lights – rising or dipping

Height of Light		HEIGHT OF EYE				
		Metres				
		1.5	3	4.6	6.1	7.6
		Feet				
		5	10	15	20	25
m	ft					
12	40	9¾	11	11¾	12½	13
15	50	10¾	11¾	12½	13¼	14
18	60	11½	12½	13½	14	14¾
21	70	12¼	13¼	14	14¾	15½
24	80	13	14	14¾	15½	16
27	90	13½	14½	15½	16	16¾
30	100	14	15	16	16½	17¼
34	110	14½	15¾	16½	17¼	17¾
37	120	15¼	16¼	17	17¾	18¼
40	130	15¾	16¾	17½	18¼	19
43	140	16¼	17¼	18	18¾	19½
46	150	16¾	17¾	18½	19¼	19¾
49	160	17	18¼	19	19¾	20¼
52	170	17½	18½	19½	20	20¾
55	180	18	19	20	20½	21¼
58	190	18½	19½	20¼	21	21½
61	200	18¾	20	20¾	21½	22
64	210	19¼	20¼	21	21¾	22½
67	220	19½	20¾	21½	22¼	22¾
70	230	20	21	22	22½	23¼
73	240	20½	21½	22¼	23	23½
76	250	20¾	21¾	22½	23¼	24
79	260	21	22¼	23	23¾	24¼
82	270	21½	22½	23¼	24	24½
85	280	21¾	23	23¾	24½	25
88	290	22	23¼	24	24¾	25¼
91	300	22½	23½	24½	25	25¾

Distance of sea horizon

Height of eye		Distance	Height of eye		Distance
metres	feet	n miles	metres	feet	n miles
0.3	1	1.15	4.3	14	4.30
0.6	2	1.62	4.9	16	4.60
0.9	3	1.99	5.5	18	4.87
1.2	4	2.30	6.1	20	5.14
1.5	5	2.57	6.7	22	5.39
1.8	6	2.81	7.3	24	5.62
2.1	7	3.04	7.9	26	5.86
2.4	8	3.25	8.5	28	6.08
2.7	9	3.45	9.1	30	6.30
3.0	10	3.63	9.8	32	6.50
3.4	11	3.81	10.4	34	6.70
3.7	12	3.98	11.0	36	6.90
4.0	13	4.14	11.6	38	7.09

Paperwork

The following paperwork should be retained on board. You will probably never be asked to show these, but you could face significant fines if they are not available when required. Some items are only necessary if going abroad. Requirements do change, so check the RYA website beforehand.

Vessel

Certificate or Registration SSR or Part 1 of the UK Ship Register.

Proof of VAT status You may also need proof that the boat was in the UK on 31 December 2020 to avoid any post-Brexit difficulties.

Short Range Certificate Your authorisation to operate a VHF radio.

Ship Radio Licence The authority to operate all the radio equipment on board.

Insurance certificate Must be an original, not a copy.

Recreational Craft Directive (Declaration of Conformity) Applies to all boats built after 16 June 1998.

Special ensign permit If applicable.

Fuel receipt Not a formal requirement, but might be needed to show that the relevant duty has been paid when abroad.

Crew

Passports Required abroad, including the Channel Islands. Make sure all are in date.

International Certificate of Competence (ICC) For skipper; may be required to be shown in some countries.

CEVNI endorsement Required if navigating EU inland waterways.

Pre-sailing checks

This is not a comprehensive list of all the checks you should carry out before sailing; that will depend on your regular maintenance routine and the actual gear fitted in your boat. You should draw up your own list for daily checks, and others for more thorough inspections of some items at longer intervals.

Running rigging
- Chafe, particularly on sheets and halyards.
- Shackle pins working loose.
- Halyards not twisted. The main halyard and topping lift are common offenders.

Standing rigging
- Split pins present and opened out correctly.
- Clevis pins secured.
- No broken strands near the terminals.
- Stay and shroud tensions 'feel' right.

Deck gear
- Nothing working loose.
- Winches free to turn.
- Anchor secured (or ready to let go, if necessary).
- Boathook available.

Safety gear
- Check lifebuoy light (if sailing at night).
- Dan buoy fully extended.
- All gear ready to deploy.

Pre-sailing checks

Engine

- Oil level – engine and gearbox.
- Coolant level.
- Weed trap clean.
- Alternator belt tension.

Seacocks

- All accessible seacock free to open/close.
- Any seacock shut which might cause flooding when heeled (galley, heads).

Log impeller

- Clean and paddle wheel free to spin (probably no need to do this unless the boat has been idle for more than a week or so, or if the readout looks suspicious).
- Check for leaks around hull fitting.

Bilges

- Dry.
- No unusual oil or other liquid under the engine.
- If there is water in the bilge, is it salt or fresh? If salt, find where it is coming from.